I0813680

TO:

FROM:

DATE:

Visit Christian Art Gifts, Inc., at www.christianartgifts.com.

Gospel Courage: 40 Days to Sharing Your Faith

Published by Christian Art Gifts, Inc., Bloomingdale, IL, USA.

The author is represented by Johnsen, Inc.

The *Gospel Courage* devotional is a companion to *Gospeler* by Willie Robertson, published by W Publishing Group, an imprint of Thomas Nelson, © 2024.

First edition 2025.

Designed by Christian Art Gifts, Inc.

Cover and interior images used under license from Shutterstock.com.

ISBN: 979-8-89678-039-7

Printed in China.

30 29 28 27 26 25
10 9 8 7 6 5 4 3 2 1

GOSPEL COURAGE

40 DAYS TO SHARING YOUR FAITH

WILLIE ROBERTSON

Christian Art PUBLISHERS

GOSPELER:

(noun) a person who zealously teaches
or professes faith in the Gospel
(The Oxford Languages Dictionary online)

Always be prepared to give an answer
to everyone who asks you to give
the reason for the hope that you have.

~1 PETER 3:15~

SO, WHERE DO WE FIND GOSPEL COURAGE?

"If there's a better way to get off this planet alive, I have not found one, other than what this Bible says."

PHIL ROBERTSON

Growing up, I heard my dad speak this truth to countless people sitting at our dinner table. He would open his Bible and read the familiar verses and passages he always shared to communicate the hope of the Gospel. At that same table, our family prayed week after week at the end of every episode of *Duck Dynasty*. Our hope was to share with viewers the same truth that changed the life of my parents. My dad heard and understood the Gospel when they were separated, and it led them to be reconciled and to commit themselves to live out their new faith. From then on, not even hunting or fishing was as important to our family as the Good News of Jesus.

Awhile back, my wife, Korie, found this old word—gospeler—pronounced *gos-SPELL-er*—and I looked up its meaning. The Oxford Languages Dictionary defines it as "a person who zealously teaches or professes faith in the Gospel." As a follower of Jesus, I know I'm called to be a gospeler. From Jesus' teaching through Paul's letters to the first churches, the New Testament is clear that anyone who follows the Lord is called to "zealously teach or profess faith in the Gospel."

In grade school, I brought my Bible with me so I could

tell my classmates about Jesus. As a teenager, I shared the Gospel with friends over pizza or in conversations on a landline phone. Today, over five decades in, I've talked to everyone from blue-collar guys in a deer stand to pro athletes in their hotel suites. I've listened to people's stories and jotted down for them the moments where their lives intersected with faith on napkins at a coffee shop or on a whiteboard at church.

I'm committed to having these conversations because my belief is that everyone needs to hear the Gospel of Jesus Christ. *What is the Gospel?* It's the good news that God loves people so much that He sent His Son, Jesus, to rescue us from sin. Jesus came to earth, died for us, was buried and raised from the dead, so we can have the gift of eternal life. This message meets sinners where we are and transforms our lives. This is the truth that my parents, my brothers, and I came to know. The truth that me and Korie, our six kids (biological and adopted), and our grandkids live by today. I believe the Bible teaches that if we *believe* the Gospel, then we should *be* His gospelers—people who proclaim the Good News to our next-door neighbor and to the ends of the earth.

If you are a follower of Jesus, you are called to share the Gospel. But you might be asking *Where do I start? How do I know what to say? Where do I find the courage?* The goal of this devotional is to help you answer those questions. In the next forty days, we will talk about how you can be prepared to give an answer for the hope you have (1 Peter 3:15). I want to help you grow in courage and confidence to tell your own story of salvation and to share the Good News of Jesus. You'll learn how to really listen to another person's story and help that person connect their experiences to the bigger story of Jesus. You'll learn where to go in the Bible to explain the Gospel, and you'll be encouraged to dig deeper into Scripture so that it shapes your conversations and your life.

When we look around at the world in these crazy times, one thing is very clear: people are searching. In all the chaos and confusion, they are desperate to find hope. They're looking for answers about this life, as well as eternity. So, if we claim to know the One who holds those answers, doesn't it make sense that we should talk about Him? That's why the Gospel is called the Good News. We have been given the privilege to share the one and only remedy for all the bad news created by sin and selfishness in this world. That's why being a gospeler is so important!

Because I want you to be successful as you start, continue through each of the forty days, and finish strong, here are a few thoughts that I hope will encourage you as you read the *Gospel Courage* devotional:

Commit to setting aside some intentional and undistracted time to go through each day. If you miss a day or two, pick back up where you left off. Don't give in to the temptation to feel any guilt; just jump back in.

Decide the best time and place in your day to read and engage. Weekends may look a bit different from your weekdays and that's fine. It's best to get away from distractions. No phones, devices, no TV, and no one else around. Focus and connect with God.

Read and take in *all* the content. I worked hard to make every word count, and God certainly did with His Word. Don't scan like you do a text or email but read each day like you would a personal letter from me.

Write down your thoughts. I've added reflection/discussion questions at the end of each day to help you connect and apply the day's content to your own life. The more open and honest you are in your answers, the more opportunity you create for growth in spiritual maturity. If you go through this devotional with a small group, you can use the questions for discussion. Whether by yourself or with others, I encourage you to write down your answers.

At the end of this journey, I hope you will take courage from what God has done in your life, that you will be better equipped to tell your own story of faith, and that you will become a *gospeler*, proclaiming the Good News of Jesus to anyone who will listen.

Willie

JESUS' COMMISSION, YOUR MISSION

As we live our lives, we carry the Gospel into the world.

I don't think I've ever met anyone who didn't want to know their purpose. God obviously hard-wired us with a desire for our lives to matter. For the folks who have figured out what they're good at or what they love, regardless of faith, we often hear things like, "I know this is what I was put on this earth to do." We all want to know why we're here. Everyone wants their lives to count.

In the Gospels, we read about the disciples, a rag-tag group of just regular folks, who followed Jesus and got to be a part of something historic and eternal. They were the ones who handed out multiplied food—starting with a handful of fish and bread and ending up with basketfuls for thousands. They saw countless people healed. They witnessed the demon-possessed get their lives back. They watched Jesus do miracles like calm a storm, call a man out of the grave, and capture the hearts of a huge crowd with His message. But after seeing all those miraculous moments, what happened when Jesus died on the cross and His body was placed in a tomb and sealed up?

When Jesus rose early on the first day of the week, He appeared first to Mary Magdalene, out of whom He had driven seven demons. She went and told those who had been with Him and who were mourning and weeping. When they heard that Jesus was alive and that she had seen

Him, they did not believe it. Afterward Jesus appeared in a different form to two of them while they were walking in the country. These returned and reported it to the rest; but they did not believe them either (Mark 16:9-13).

Most of the disciples were grieving and weeping and wouldn't believe that Jesus had actually done what He said He would do. Sometimes it's hard for us to remember that they were just ordinary people. They weren't some specially created group of superheroes. In fact, most of the twelve were men no one would pick to be on their A-team. But Jesus did. Now, after His death, they were thinking all was lost and their new-found purpose was over. They didn't believe their own friends who had given them eyewitness reports that Jesus was alive. Luke 24:11 even says, "But the story sounded like nonsense to the men, so they didn't believe it" (NLT).

In John chapters 20 and 21, we're told about encounters the disciples eventually had with the risen Jesus. There was evidently some unfinished business, especially with Peter, and Jesus wanted to spend a few moments with the eleven that remained. Sure, Jesus had taught them how to care for people, feed crowds, and meet needs, but helping people is only the beginning of the mission. That was important for the disciples to know and still is for us today.

In the final verses of Matthew's Gospel, Jesus gave the disciples the purpose for the rest of their lives: He commissioned them into God's work on earth in His name—a movement so strong, we are a part of it two thousand years later. A mission to not only accept the gift of Jesus, but offer that gift to others, giving them a whole new mission as well. The Good News is meant to spread and grow as it moves through each generation.

Then the eleven disciples left for Galilee, going to the mountain where Jesus had told them to go. When they found Him, they worshiped Him—though some of them doubted! Jesus came and told His disciples, "I have been given all authority in heaven and on earth. Therefore, go and make disciples of all the nations, baptizing them in the name of the Father and the Son and the Holy Spirit. Teach these new disciples to obey all the commands I have given you. And be sure of this: I am with you always, even to the end of the age," (Matthew 28:16-20).

What always strikes me is that there was worship but also doubt. It's amazing they were looking at someone who had risen from the dead, who they knew as a friend for years, and still had some doubts. This is a reminder that God can use all of us—even when there is doubt, fear, or a lack of enthusiasm—for His purpose. Regardless, Jesus didn't feel the need to go back to square one. He just gave them the mission right where they were at the time. Jesus reminded the disciples that what He was saying was coming directly from God as He gave them their calling, purpose, meaning, their "why you matter," and "what you were put on this earth to do." His three commands were:

1. Make disciples of all nations
2. Baptize those disciples in the name of the Father, Son, and Holy Spirit
3. Teach them about Me (Jesus)

Now, here's some really great news about the meaning of our lives and our purpose: Those exact commands and promises that Jesus gave His disciples right before He returned to Heaven are made to us today. This is for us as well. We get to follow an incredible legacy of world changers in the faith.

If you have been searching for your authentic purpose and meaning in life—this is it! Being a person who delights in God's goodness and proclaims it to everyone who will listen is what God intended when He made you. Of course, we are all going to lead different lives and have unique stories, but the ultimate calling and mission are the same. As we go through life, we carry the Gospel into the world, sharing who Jesus is and what He can do, because of what He has already done for us. We make disciples, baptize, and teach, because He is with us everywhere we go and in anything we do.

Whether or not you had any idea that this same mission was part of the life to which you are called, right here, on our first day, I want to be sure you know it's the final answer to the question, "Why am I here?"

REFLECTION QUESTIONS

Up to this moment, have you felt like you knew your purpose in life? If so, what is it?

How does a clear understanding of Jesus' commands to you as His follower affect your thoughts and feelings about your life and future?

CONVERTING CONVERSATIONS

When someone accepts the Good News, there is nothing quite like that feeling.

When my dad and mom (Phil and Kay) started their journey together with Jesus and agreed that God would be the center of their marriage, that choice was a game changer for our entire family. While I was just a little guy at the time, I often think about how different life might have been had they not heard the Gospel. Or if they did hear it and chose not to believe.

My aunt Jan, Dad's sister, had a very strong faith. She loved my parents and us kids. Jan hated seeing what her brother's choices were doing to our family. So, she went to her pastor in West Monroe, Louisiana—a man named Bill Smith—and asked him to go talk to her wayward brother. Now, every day people go to their pastors and ask them to talk to someone. The typical answer might be something like, "Well, invite them to church on Sunday and I'll be glad to visit with them at the altar call or after church." Or maybe, "Sure, have them reach out to my secretary and we'll schedule an appointment."

But Aunt Jan made it clear to Pastor Bill that Dad was not going to set foot in any church, so he would have to go to him. She asked Bill to go talk to Dad at an interesting place—the bar he owned and managed. Still open to helping Jan, he asked, "Okay, which bar in town is it?" Jan answered, "Well, it's not here. It's in southern Arkansas, about an hour away."

All of us Robertsons thank God that Pastor Bill was willing to take the time and the risk to drive to a bar in another state to tell a man who might never be able to do anything for him or his church about the Good News of Jesus. As you can tell by the story, Bill overcame a lot of the usual barriers we can use as excuses to not share Jesus. But the one thing my Aunt Jan said to Pastor Bill that may have made a difference: "If you convert Phil Robertson, he'll convert a thousand."

All these years later, it's been a thousand alright, thousands of times over. Whether one person at our kitchen table or a massive crowd in an arena, on our TV show or his podcast, countless people have heard and received the Gospel from Phil Robertson. That's the legacy that Korie and I and our own family are carrying out in our lives today.

Pastor Bill's conversation with my dad reminds me of when Peter met Jesus. That first encounter would immediately get any fisherman's attention. I know it got mine! Jesus was preaching to a large crowd on the shoreline, while Peter, James, and John were nearby washing out their nets from an all-nighter where they were skunked—catching absolutely no fish. Seeing two empty boats and knowing the water would be a natural way to better carry His voice to the crowd, Jesus stepped into one of the boats and asked Peter to push it out a little further into the water. Peter immediately did what the Lord asked without any questions. When Jesus was done teaching the crowd,

He turned His focus to Peter, giving him a really interesting instruction.

> *When he had finished speaking, he said to Simon, "Put out into deep water, and let down the nets for a catch." Simon answered, "Master, we've worked hard all night and haven't caught anything. But because you say so, I will let down the nets."*
>
> LUKE 5:4-5

While Peter didn't argue with the Lord, he did qualify his answer with a polite, "just in case you missed it, we did spend all night trying." Yet, what was about to happen was the first of many times Peter would witness Jesus make a whole lot out of little to nothing.

> *When they had done so, they caught such a large number of fish that their nets began to break. So they signaled their partners in the other boat to come and help them, and they came and filled both boats so full that they began to sink.*
>
> LUKE 5:6-7

As a kid, the first time I read how Jesus blessed some exhausted fishermen with a boatful after a bad night, I knew I was all-in. But that's when the story gets even bigger and better than just a good catch. Peter's life was about to change forever. Just like my parents, my brothers, and me.

When Simon Peter saw this, he fell at Jesus' knees and said, "Go away from me, Lord; I am a sinful man!" For he and all his companions were astonished at the catch of fish they had taken, and so were James and John, the sons of Zebedee, Simon's partners. Then Jesus said to Simon, "Don't be afraid; from now on you will fish for people." So they pulled their boats up on shore, left everything and followed him.

LUKE 5:8-11

Even as a kid, I also knew that "fishing for people" was hard work. I had seen that in my parents' lives. You need to study Scripture. You have to care about folks, dedicating a lot of time and patience. But also, much like pulling a big fish up out of the water, when someone accepts the Good News, there is nothing quite like that feeling. The "catch" is part of what gives us courage to carry on fishing.

REFLECTION QUESTIONS

What can we learn about caring for people by how Jesus used a bad night of fishing to reach Peter, James, and John?

Fishing is a good analogy for being a gospeler, but how might your work or career be used to become a way for you to help others hear and understand the Gospel?

SO, WHAT ARE YOU?

I'm not sure what my job is, exactly.

As Christians, we can be quick to excuse ourselves from any responsibility of telling others about our faith in Jesus. There will always be a list of reasons why we can't or won't share, but in these forty days, I want to attempt to tell you how *you* can and why *you* should. Maybe it's simply that you have been a little confused about who you are in the Kingdom of God and what role you play. You may be saying, *I'm not sure what my job is, exactly.* So, let's look at some misconceptions and terms used to describe certain jobs, some that are in the Bible and some that aren't.

We are therefore Christ's ambassadors,
as though God were making his appeal
through us. We implore you on
Christ's behalf: Be reconciled to God.

2 CORINTHIANS 5:20

Paul says we are called to be Christ's "ambassadors" here on this earth. The role of an ambassador is to promote or represent something or someone. The U.S. sends ambassadors all over the world to speak for the government in foreign countries. I'm sure it's common knowledge that if you represent America, you are expected to actually talk about America. In fact, that's the whole reason for the job. Most folks who have ever held that position have been honored to hold the title.

I mentioned to a friend one time about an evangelism class I was teaching at my church. He told me that the word *evangelism* was scary to him, conjuring up an old-timey religious vibe that he did not like. I had never heard someone say that before. No one had ever told me that just the word *evangelism* turned them off. Not sure what to think, I wondered, *Maybe I should steer away from using that particular word.* Later on, another person mentioned that the word was not in the Bible. And what do you know? I checked and it's not!

I was beginning to understand that the terms we use today in Christianity may actually matter to people. As I taught the class, I had some people tell me they didn't come because they thought evangelism only had to do with missionary work. They had assumed that people who try and convert the lost only do that sort of thing overseas. I soon realized I was up against far more than I had originally thought when it comes to sharing our faith with others. People were putting their own preconceived ideas to the word *evangelism*, which maybe made it easier to "opt out" based on what they thought it meant. Helping folks become gospelers was definitely going to be a challenge. So much so that even the word *gospeler* had literally vanished from our language. Throughout the years since Jesus came to this earth, there have been many religious terms created and used to describe almost everything and everybody. Today, we seem to have a label for any train of thought out there. But, to be a gospeler is simply to always have the name of Jesus on your lips.

Through Jesus, therefore, let us continually offer to God a sacrifice of praise—the fruit of lips that openly profess his name.

HEBREWS 13:15

As an example, I've been married for thirty-plus years, and you don't have to talk to me or my wife very long without us referencing each other in some way. It becomes second nature to talk about someone with whom you have a great relationship.

So Christ himself gave the apostles, the prophets, the evangelists, the pastors and teachers, to equip his people for works of service, so that the body of Christ may be built up until we all reach unity in the faith and in the knowledge of the Son of God and become mature, attaining to the whole measure of the fullness of Christ.

EPHESIANS 4:11-13

Evangelists are mentioned in this passage as a gift from Jesus. I have had the privilege of seeing many gifted people who have a powerful way of preaching the Gospel to the lost. While they may have a true spiritual gift, that doesn't make the rest of us exempt from just telling others about the One who changed our lives. It doesn't prevent us from studying God's Word to help us better know and understand the message of Jesus so we can share with people.

We can all live on mission and be missionaries, maybe not in foreign lands, but right in our own neighborhoods, workplaces, and communities. Evangelism is simply getting the word out about Jesus to all those we come in contact with through our daily lives. We can all be evangelists or gospelers. Maybe not to big crowds, but if you bring only one person to the Lord, you are an evangelist to him or her. All of us who say we know Jesus are ambassadors of Jesus Christ who help people when they are in need and spread the word of who they represent.

So, don't get too caught up in terms, especially when you feel they can disqualify you from carrying out the Great Commission of Jesus Christ. I believe the evil one loves it when followers of Jesus keep their mouths closed about the Gospel. Preachers may preach to their churches, but when the whole church starts preaching, revival is on the way. As a Christian, because you have the Gospel in you, you can start getting the Good News out to others.

REFLECTION QUESTIONS

Have you ever disqualified yourself or opted out from sharing your faith because you thought it wasn't "your gift"?

What are some practical steps you could take to either start or improve being an ambassador for Christ?

SEARCH AND RESCUE

The majority of Jesus' contact with people was one-on-one, up-close-and-personal moments.

When a person is presumed to be lost and in trouble, search and rescue begins. Because of the many different places people can go missing, there are first responders that know how to search in the woods, water, mountains, and from the air. They jump into action to try and find the person as quickly as possible. In any of those situations, *search* is the action, but *rescue* is the goal.

There's a strong chance that, like me, you aren't trained to be on a search and rescue team. That said, if someone we love goes missing, of course, we would do everything possible to find them. But what about people we don't know? What if a first responder asked you for help to find a total stranger? Let's be honest, lots of folks would answer, "Sorry, I'm not trained for that. And I don't know who this person is anyway, so I'll leave it to the professionals."

Like we talked about yesterday, it's interesting how we can take that same mindset about sharing the Gospel. Yet, Scripture teaches us that those who follow Jesus are also team members on His spiritual search and rescue mission. Besides sharing Him with our family and friends who don't know the Good News, there are going to be times when God does prompt us to talk to people we don't know. For example, there's the conversation with a new neighbor or coworker, someone who sits next to us on a plane and starts talking, or a person we meet at a social gathering who asks the usual small-talk questions about our lives. There are so many everyday examples of situations that can present open doors for the Gospel.

There will even be times we realize we are talking to someone who has no idea he or she even needs salvation. In the Gospels, we read how Jesus encountered a lot of folks who didn't know they were lost and needed Him. That is, until they experienced who He was. A great example was a small guy with a big bank account and a bad reputation named Zacchaeus.

As a dishonest, despised, and disrespected tax collector, when Zacchaeus found out that Jesus was coming to Jericho, he was curious enough to climb up into a tree to get a good seat. But just being a spectator soon turned into a face-to-face.

> *When Jesus came by, he looked up at Zacchaeus and called him by name. "Zacchaeus!" he said. "Quick, come down! I must be a guest in your home today." Zacchaeus quickly climbed down and took Jesus to his house in great excitement and joy.*
>
> LUKE 19:5-6 NLT

For Zacchaeus, the outcast suddenly felt like a celebrity. For probably the first time in his life, someone important had acknowledged and chosen him. As for the crowd, they didn't seem to understand what Jesus was doing, much less why He was doing it.

But the people were displeased. "He has gone to be the guest of a notorious sinner," they grumbled.

LUKE 19:7 NLT

While a lot of the folks outside were busy pointing fingers, inside, after talking with Jesus, the tax collector had a sudden change of heart.

Meanwhile, Zacchaeus stood before the Lord and said, "I will give half my wealth to the poor, Lord, and if I have cheated people on their taxes, I will give them back four times as much!"

LUKE 19:8 NLT

It's interesting that Zacchaeus didn't actually ask Jesus to save him, but he was obviously convicted that his life needed to change. He openly confessed and repented of everything he had done. His first step of faith in Jesus was to commit to two huge actions: First, give half his wealth to the poor and, second—with the other half—pay back everyone he had cheated four times the original amount. So, how did Jesus respond? Did He say, "Whoa, now hold on, Zach! You're going to need to bow your head, close your eyes, and pray the sinner's prayer first." No, instead:

Jesus responded, "Salvation has come to this home today, for this man has shown himself to be a true son of Abraham. For the Son of Man came to seek and save those who are lost."

LUKE 19:9-10 NLT

Reading through the Gospels, while Jesus did preach to large crowds at times, the majority of His contact with people was one-on-one, up-close-and-personal moments. From the Pharisee Nicodemus to the woman at the well, from a Roman centurion to a demon-possessed man, Jesus was constantly on a search and rescue mission to "seek and save those who are lost." There's nothing that tells us Zacchaeus climbed up in the tree because he knew he needed what Jesus had. That didn't happen until after a Gospel conversation.

I've found there seems to be quite a few Christians today that, like Zacchaeus up in the tree, just want a good seat for the show on Sundays. Going to Heaven and getting blessed appears to be the only thing they feel like they "signed up for." But here's the issue: We are all following the same Jesus that went after a guy like Zacchaeus to bring him into His kingdom. That means we are also called to be part of His search and rescue mission by having one-on-one conversations about Him. Why? Because Jesus still comes "to seek and save those who are lost." In fact, the abundant life that He promised in John 10 can only be found when we decide to give Jesus to others, not focus on what we can get from Jesus. The very truth that Zacchaeus discovered.

REFLECTION QUESTIONS

Do you tend to treat the Gospel like something you should keep to yourself or something you need to give away?

Whatever your answer, how do you think your mindset about the Gospel has affected your faith up to now?

GO TO WHO YOU KNOW

While we should be going into every nation, we could start right here at home.

While this book will help with talking to strangers, like Jesus with Zacchaeus, I don't want you to only think about being ready to share with random people who you might bump into throughout life. Jesus told His disciples to go make other disciples in all the nations, but we need to remember we should start close to home first. Sometimes we need to just go to those we know best and make sure they have the Good News.

I was at a conference one time on global evangelism. One of the leaders was talking about taking the Gospel into all nations, especially ones where there are very few Christians or where the Gospel is not being preached at all. While I was completely on board with the heart of the message and believe that to be very true, I raised my hand with a question, "How can we go to scary places that speak completely different languages to preach the Good News when we don't really do a good job telling others here at home where it's relatively safe and most folks speak English?" My point was, while we should be going into every nation, we could start right here at home.

When my daughter, Sadie, was around nineteen years old, she and Korie were traveling the country on a tour bus, away from home for several weeks, telling others about the Gospel. Now, I am the main cook of our house, and I was not on the bus. So, these ladies were going to have to figure out the food situation on their own. One night, they decided to make a simple dip to go with chips. Korie had the expertise and asked Sadie to open up some beans, handing her a can opener. My daughter kept awkwardly putting the tool on the can until they both broke out laughing. They realized she had no idea how to actually use a can opener. She had never opened one that didn't have a pull tab. Of all the thousands of meals I have prepared with her in the house, I had never shown her how to actually use a can opener.

After hearing that story about my daughter, even as the family chef, I wasn't so focused on passing down kitchen skills. I was glad that Sadie could see the big picture, that she got the main thing I wanted to pass on to my kids—how to share the Gospel of Jesus Christ. In Matthew 28, when Jesus said to go, He said to start in Jerusalem. We can start by sharing at home. Then, we go to the rest of our family. Next, to our friends. Then to our work. There are so many places we can go to share right now that aren't far from where we live.

One of my favorite Bible stories is in Acts 16 about a jailer. After he witnesses the faith of Paul and Silas who chose to worship while in prison and stay put even when the cell doors were flung open, the jailer brings the two gospelers to his house. He wants to be saved by whoever had saved them, but he also includes his entire household in hearing this Good News. And what happens? They *all* get saved in the middle of the night! We'll dive deeper into that story on a later day, but I want to draw your attention now to the fact that the jailer went to his family first after he witnessed some Jesus-inspired miracles.

Back before that, in Matthew 9, we read about the moment Matthew the tax collector chooses to follow Jesus. (Another story we'll get into later.) What does he do? He invites all his friends over to meet Jesus.

While Jesus was having dinner at
Matthew's house, many tax collectors
and sinners came and ate
with him and his disciples.
When the Pharisees saw this,
they asked his disciples,
"Why does your teacher eat
with tax collectors and sinners?"

MATTHEW 9:10-11

Just like how the jailer got his family together, Matthew invited his friends to hear the Messiah teach. Sometimes the lowest hanging fruit is right in front of us. We just need to have the courage to share with them. I know this can be difficult for people, not because we know them, but, rather, because they know us. A roadblock that can hold us back from sharing with the ones we love most is the fact that they have seen our messy lives before Jesus took over. Strangers don't really know us and might even think we are kind and generous to share with them. But with our family and friends, we may fear they'll respond with, "Really? Now, you're getting all holy on us?" Don't let that hold you back, because the message is too important. Use those moments to tell your story. Live your life in such a way that they can't help but notice something is different about you now. And what's different is that Jesus has taken over your life.

REFLECTION QUESTIONS

If you begin to share what Jesus has done for you with your friends and family, how do you think they would react? What's your plan if someone is negative toward you?

Take a few minutes to write down the names of people you know who really need to hear the Good News.

JESUS' MASTER CLASS ON CONVERSATIONS

— PART 1 —

We need to go where the person's story leads, always pointing to Jesus as the answer.

Most every day, you have conversations. Once you have the desire to help people better understand Jesus, you'll want to start steering those towards the Gospel. But exactly how do you do that without sounding strange or weird or awkward? One of the many reasons I love studying the Bible is to see how people had these conversations so long ago. After all, the first followers of Jesus changed the world and, frankly, my life, by how they lived and what they taught. A long time ago I had to make the decision to let the Bible lead me, through God's Spirit, in how to have these conversations. I also had to decide that if someone thinks I'm weird for wanting to talk about Jesus, then that's okay with me. Those are two decisions you will have to make also.

Today and tomorrow, we'll go to John chapter 4 to hear the Master Himself give a Master Class on how to have a conversation, offering us the best example of how to be a gospeler. These two days are crucial to see how Jesus guides someone from a mundane transaction to a miraculous transformation that starts with one person and ends with many others coming to know Him. (Exactly the purpose of this book.) Jesus would often begin right where a person was in the moment and then walk him or her to where he or she needed to go.

Over the years, I have talked to many people who had no idea about Jesus. In those situations, we can easily be tempted to think we have to come up with some big opening spiritual question to start talking about the Gospel. But how about something as simple as, "Will you give me a drink of water?"

Jesus' disciples had gone to buy food, so He was alone and walking through a certain region of Samaria. Around noon, He stopped to rest beside a water well on the outskirts of a town. When a woman came to fill her jar to take it back home, the conversation began ...

Jesus said to her,
"Will you give me a drink?"
JOHN 4:7

First, notice the obvious—the place where Jesus asked the question was at a well where she had come for water. It wasn't random or awkward. It was practical. He's thirsty and she came to draw water up with her jar. He asked for a drink. That was it. This shows us how easy a conversation can happen.

In the culture back in that day, there were three reasons why a Jewish man might not have even acknowledged or spoken to her. Number one, she was a woman. Number two, she was a Samaritan. And number three, she appeared to have a questionable reputation. The tradition of the day was for women of the town to go to the well together early in the morning for their daily supply of water. Along the way, they would talk and catch up. For some reason, this particular woman came later in the day and alone. In spite of these reasons to keep His distance, Jesus showed that He cared more about her life than the culture or what anyone thought. He didn't just look for an opportunity, He made an opportunity. Think about it, if you don't really care, why would you ask anything about anyone's life? But soon, He began to steer the conversation to His mission:

The Samaritan woman said to him,
"You are a Jew and I am a Samaritan woman.
How can you ask me for a drink?"
(For Jews do not associate with Samaritans.) Jesus
answered her, "If you knew the gift of God and who
it is that asks you for a drink, you would have asked
him and he would have given you living water."
"Sir," the woman said, "you have nothing to
draw with and the well is deep. Where can you
get this living water? Are you greater than our
father Jacob, who gave us the well and drank from
it himself, as did also his sons and his livestock?"
Jesus answered, "Everyone who drinks this
water will be thirsty again, but whoever drinks
the water I give them will never thirst. Indeed,
the water I give them will become in them
a spring of water welling up to eternal life."

JOHN 4:9-14

At first, she had no idea what He was saying. While Jesus is using words like *gifts*, *living water*, and *eternal life*, she is looking for buckets, ladles, and earthly ancestors. The application for us is when gathering someone's story, don't be surprised when the person has no clue what Jesus is all about. I never expect people who don't know Him to act or talk like people who do. Plus, when most folks can't see or feel something "real," they tend to quickly get disinterested. They ask questions like, "Can this help with my bills?" or "Can this get my kids to behave?" This is why we have to move the person beyond what can be seen and felt at the moment to believing in something that cannot be seen, moving from sight to faith.

While this lady is telling Jesus all she knows about this well and its water, He begins to move from the earthly to the spiritual. Notice that no matter what she says, He stays on topic. This brings up another really important point for us to understand about Gospel conversations: Jesus didn't say the same thing to every person. There was no formula. He had no script. This was a tailor-made, personalized conversation just for this lady. When we talk about the Gospel, we may feel like we have to say exactly the right thing to the person. We may even try and offer a one-size-fits-all message. But, following Jesus' example, we need to go where the person's story leads, always pointing to Him as the answer.

There are several important takeaways from this:

- Jesus started with an opening question in context with the situation that made practical sense.

- Jesus tied His original question to the Good News.
- Jesus didn't have any assumptions that she would know who He was.
- Jesus stayed on topic, no matter what she said.

Tomorrow, we'll continue the conversation with this woman to see how Jesus led her to the Truth.

REFLECTION QUESTIONS

In what ways does today's story help you see how talking about the Gospel can begin in a very natural way?

____

____

____

____

____

What can you learn from the fact that Jesus crossed so many cultural boundaries to reach this woman?

____

____

____

____

____

JESUS' MASTER CLASS ON CONVERSATIONS

— PART 2 —

We need to ask questions to allow the person to give us as much of their story as possible, so we can help as much as we can with answers.

Yesterday, we left off the story of Jesus and the woman at the well with Him explaining what He meant by "living water." At that point, the woman seems like she is beginning to understand:

> *Sir, give me this water so that I won't get thirsty and have to keep coming here to draw water.*
>
> JOHN 4:15

Notice that she is now asking Jesus for something. This is a crucial turning point in their conversation. She's intrigued and wants to know more. She sounds open to doing whatever is necessary to receive what He's offering. There is also some indication that she knows her life is not where it needs to be. All these signs point to the best-case scenario when sharing the Gospel with someone. She asks. Nothing is forced. Jesus was always a gentleman and never pushed Himself on anyone. He always offered a choice, which is exactly what we do.

When the woman asked Jesus for the living water, she still didn't understand what it was or who was telling her at the time. By now, the original request for a drink of water seems to fade. Jesus knows it is time to take the conversation deeper and more personal.

He told her, "Go, call your husband and come back."
"I have no husband," she replied.

JOHN 4:16-17

An important point here is that, as God, Jesus is omniscient and we, obviously, are not. He knows everything, all the details of this woman's life, which means He also knew exactly what to say and what questions to ask. Because we don't have that advantage, we need to ask questions to allow the person to give us as much of their story as possible. Why? Just so we can know? No, so their story can guide us to help as much as we can with answers.

Often, when we are talking to people, we may know something about their life and their past. Maybe that's led to why we are talking to them in the first place. Over the years, I've had many mamas bring me their children to talk to, along with a laundry list of behaviors that are not Christlike. For any of us, we have to deal with where we are before we can decide we need to change. With the woman at the well, Jesus is getting all the bad information out, knowing she will then begin to understand how much better her life can be with Him. At this point, He starts to reveal His identity:

Jesus said to her, "You are right when you say you
have no husband. The fact is, you have had five

husbands, and the man you now have is not your husband. What you have just said is quite true."

John 4:17-18

Because Jesus had literally gone out of His way to help this woman, we know He was not trying to embarrass her. Here is where I see another big difference in what Jesus did and what we often do. At this point, we may decide it's time to wrap it up, pray, and then tell the person they've got Jesus. But, following His example, we have to go to the next level to hear the whole story. Jesus wanted her to get out her issues and struggles to deal with them. He only had her best interest at heart. Nothing she shared would repel Him, like perhaps it had with many of the people she knew. Jesus wrote the playbook for redemption, so He knew that He had to help this woman deal with her past, so she could walk into her future.

While she didn't lie to Him, she also didn't tell Him the whole truth either. That makes sense because she had just met Him. Jesus is telling her that He already knows the details of her life and still cares enough to talk to her and help. He wants her to see for herself that He is the Living Water who will revolutionize her life. Jesus wants to hear her entire story, while showing that nothing she says will affect His love for her, unlike the other men in her life. Finally, her moment of truth arrived.

The woman said, "I know that Messiah" (called Christ) "is coming. When he comes, he will explain everything to us." Then Jesus declared,

"I, the one speaking to you—I am he."

JOHN 4:25-26

What happened next? She became a gospeler!

Many of the Samaritans from that town believed in him because of the woman's testimony, "He told me everything I ever did." So when the Samaritans came to him, they urged him to stay with them, and he stayed two days. And because of his words many more became believers. They said to the woman, "We no longer believe just because of what you said; now we have heard for ourselves, and we know that this man really is the Savior of the world."

JOHN 4:39-42

One important detail in this story we shouldn't miss is in verse 28: "Then, leaving her water jar, the woman went back to the town." She left her physical water behind when she experienced the Living Water.

Here are a few more important takeaways from this conversation:

- Jesus moved from the earthly to the spiritual, all while sticking to His opening topic.
- Jesus moved from what she could do for Him to what He could do for her.
- Jesus customized the message to her and her circumstances but never compromised the truth.
- Jesus ended up at the same conclusion as all His

stories—to focus on Heaven, not earth, and to please God, not men.

There can be many different ways to get the story of Jesus to others. While listening to the countless issues that folks struggle with, the answer to what everyone is looking for is found in the Gospel. No matter how the conversations begin, we can always trust that He can solve everyone's sin problem. Even when we start with a simple question.

REFLECTION QUESTIONS

How does Jesus' conversation with the woman at the well encourage you in how to have your own Gospel conversations?

____

____

____

____

Of the bullet points from yesterday and today, what takeaways speak to you the most?

____

____

____

____

THE CHALLENGE IN THE CHOICE

If you are a believer in Jesus, He has given you a message to share.

When I arrived at a conference I had been invited to attend, I knew very few details about the event. I didn't really know if I would enjoy it or if the information I would hear would be useful to me. The strategy I came up with was to just quietly slip in the back door of a few sessions after they started, try to stay under the radar, and get a feel for what the guest speakers were covering. Since I was staying in the same hotel where the conference was held, my plan was if I decided I wasn't interested, I could just sneak out, go back to my room, and catch up on some business.

On the morning of the first session, I asked someone at the registration table for a schedule of who was speaking and the topics that would be covered. The person gave me a link to pull up the information on my phone. As I scanned through the schedule, the speakers, and the topics, when I got to the afternoon session, guess who was the first speaker after lunch? Me! Yep, there was my name on the schedule. Unless there was some other guy there named Willie Robertson, I was speaking in a few hours!

Someone on the leadership team had invited me and I had accepted. But there was just one problem. They never told me I was a guest speaker. I assumed I was just a guest, and they assumed if I was coming, I was speaking. Thankfully, I saw the schedule in enough time to try and start figuring out what I was going to do.

That story reminds me of one of my favorite verses—1 Peter 3:15.

> *But in your hearts revere Christ as Lord. Always be prepared to give an answer to everyone who asks you to give the reason for the hope that you have.*

Now that we have talked about our commission as followers of Jesus and the Gospel conversations He had and can lead us to have, the next question is: When do we share? When will these take place? Let's dive a little deeper into what Peter tells us in the verse you just read:

- Who is Christ? ... Lord.
- When do we need to be prepared to share about Him? ... Always.
- What do we give people who ask? ... An answer about Him.
- Who do we give an answer about Jesus? ... Everyone who asks.
- What do we tell them? ... The reason He is our hope.

At the event I just told you about, there was no chance I would tell the host I wasn't going to speak because they had failed to let me know I was one of the speakers. Even though the conference was not my expertise, I knew I could tell my story. No matter what an event is about, I am always willing to tell folks the reason for the hope that I have in Jesus. That message works anywhere or in any conversation I have with others. I may not be prepared to speak on a certain topic, but I'm always prepared to talk about the Gospel. Why? Because Jesus gave me a gift. Not a gift of speaking on short notice, but the gift of eternal life. I take that gift and give it back to others as my gift to them. I took the fact that they wanted me to speak as a sign from Him that there was something these people needed to hear. Even if it wasn't on the original agenda, it could be now. When Jesus asked for a drink from the woman at the well, she had no idea where the conversation was headed, but He did. He was prepared. And so was I.

As gospelers, we never know when the Lord is going to call our name to have a conversation with someone about Him. We never know when He will put someone in our path that needs to hear the Gospel. If you are a believer in Jesus, He has given you a message to share, "an answer" that "gives the reason for the hope that you have." An answer that people need to hear.

If you ask yourself, "Do I feel ready to share? Am I prepared?" and your honest answer is no, that's not a reason to start beating yourself up. It just means you have to begin moving in a new direction to get ready. That's the goal of this devotional—to be a daily step in the right direction. To get prepared and stay prepared. To be able to share your own story of salvation. To know how to talk through the basics of the Good News. To point people to

Jesus through the truth of Scripture. To accomplish these, we have to commit to digging into the Bible and learning how to present the Good News. Being effective at sharing the Gospel takes a lot of practice. Like me at that conference, God will give you the opportunity to speak, once you commit and start your preparation.

REFLECTION QUESTIONS

What is your takeaway from 1 Peter 3:15?

What are your thoughts on the questions, "Do I feel ready to share? Am I prepared?" How do you feel about getting ready for these opportunities that God wants to give you?

PATIENCE IN THE PROCESS

We have to take the time to listen to someone's story.

In Day 5, I shared a little-known fact about me—I love to cook for my family every chance I get. There are two aspects that I really enjoy about starting from scratch and serving a great meal to the people I love: the preparation and the process. These are probably the two things that most people hate about cooking, but they're actually what I enjoy most, way more than even eating the food!

First, I have to decide what I'm going to cook. What meat or fish? How many vegetables? What kind of bread? Am I going to serve a dessert? Then I have to be sure of what I already have in my pantry and fridge. Second, I have to make a list of what I need and go shop for those items. Before I ever get out a pan or a pot or turn on a stove or fire up a grill, I have to walk through my prep work. Finally, no matter what I choose to cook, there's always a very specific process for each food on the menu. There's an order to everything I do. Timing is a huge part of every meal to be sure something isn't ready too soon or too late. When I start cooking, I can't just dump everything in a pot. I might have to sauté the meat first, then add some veggies, or rice, or stock, and then, of course, plenty of seasoning. Like I said, for me, the process is definitely where I have the most fun.

As we move through each day in this book, you are

going to see that preparation and process are just as important in learning to share the Gospel as they are for me in cooking and serving a meal for my family. Both preparation and the process take a lot of grace. You'll need to be patient with yourself as you prepare, but then you'll also have to be patient with anyone who walks with you through the process of sharing and hearing the Gospel.

When I think back to all the people I've shared the Good News with—from my first times as a kid in grade school all the way to last week—every time begins the same way—with a conversation. I have to take the time to listen to the person's story. Then I have to ask good questions to understand where the person is and what is needed. I have to pay attention to the moments in life where they may have been stuck or hurt and respond to those. You can't move to the next step until the person is ready. You can't get distracted talking about getting baptized or joining a church if the person is struggling with the need for repentance and forgiveness. Or if they are dealing with basic truths like believing Jesus is who He said He is. Like they say, you can't put your cart before your horse.

Consider the woman at the well again. She needed a bit of nudging to get out the whole story. In any conversation, after some questions, you may discover that the person had a bad experience at a church or with someone who claimed to be a Christian but who hurt them. Maybe they feel like they've messed up too much. Maybe they're angry at God. Whatever the issue might be, we need to listen and let them know how much we care about what they are sharing.

As we hear someone's story, along with the pain, baggage, and mistakes, we have to find a way to move the conversation to faith. We can't stop just because someone says they go to church or was baptized as a kid. In fact, at some point, it's good to just ask directly, "Do you believe you have a relationship with Jesus?" There will always be three answers: "Yes," "No," or "I'm not sure." Any of those responses can lead to more questions as you dig through their faith story.

In Ephesians 6, following the legendary armor of God passage, Paul talked about this very dynamic in sharing the Gospel with people. He asked the church at Ephesus to pray that he would have the right words to be able to explain the Good News.

Pray in the Spirit at all times and on every occasion.
Stay alert and be persistent in your prayers
for all believers everywhere. And pray for me, too.
Ask God to give me the right words so I can
boldly explain God's mysterious plan that the
Good News is for Jews and Gentiles alike. I am
in chains now, still preaching this message as
God's ambassador. So pray that I will keep
on speaking boldly for him, as I should.

EPHESIANS 6:18-20 NLT

Now, remember, this is Paul the apostle here, the guy who wrote more books in the New Testament than anyone else, planted churches all over the known world, and preached to thousands. So, why would he ask the church to pray for his ability to share the Gospel? He literally knew the truth better than anyone on the planet. The answer for him is the same answer for you and me, found in verse 18: "at all times and on every occasion." Paul knew he couldn't do *anything* outside of the Holy Spirit. He wanted God to give him *specifically* what each person he spoke with needed to understand about Jesus. He wanted people to experience "God's mysterious plan" through "God's ambassador." That can happen for us when we submit to His preparation and His process through the Spirit for the sake of the Gospel.

REFLECTION QUESTIONS

How might separating your experience of sharing the Gospel into two stages—preparation and process—help you simplify your approach?

How does Paul's request for prayer to have "the right words" and to "keep on speaking boldly for him" encourage you to rely less on yourself and more on God's Spirit?

LEARNING TO LISTEN

I don't jump to provide an answer without finding out about the person's life.

A few years back, I helped a local church start a ministry for anyone who came to a service on Sunday mornings and wanted to know more about the Gospel. I had trained a few folks in the way that I share the Good News—exactly what I am taking you through. One Sunday morning, I was in the room just after the first service had started. A young lady slowly opened the door, stuck her head in, and asked, "What is this?" I think she must have been curious about the small sign above the door that said, "First Step." This was a rare time when someone dropped by *during* church and didn't wait until afterwards. I answered her, "This is the place you can take the first step toward Jesus Christ." Fairly loud, she responded by saying, "Oh s***!" I just laughed and said, "Come on in, you may need to hear this."

After telling me her name, she let me know that this was the first time she had ever set foot in a church building. Invited by her neighbors, after the music ended, she had become bored and decided to go explore. I asked her if she would mind sharing her story with me and she quickly opened up about a very troubled past. When she finished, like always, I started writing key words from Bible passages on the whiteboard and drawing out the aspects of the Gospel. While she didn't know much about the Lord, she was listening intently.

Much like the woman at the well, she was very confused at first by all the spiritual talk. She also had some presumed ideas about God. Just like I learned from Jesus, I was showing that I cared and was willing to talk with her. Even though we came from completely different backgrounds and had met by chance, after hearing her story, I gave her the Good News in the simplest way I could.

About the time I was done, the service let out and her neighbors looked into the room, "Oh! There you are!" I smiled and told them how we had a great talk. She then said, "This guy told me about Jesus, the Holy Spirit, and .... uh, one more, but I can't remember the last one." Before the young lady left, I made sure she knew I had no judgment about her story. I told her if she ever wanted to come back, she was always welcome. She smiled and nodded as the neighbors thanked me.

Over the years, some of my favorite TV shows have been *My 600 Pound Life* and *Dr. Phil*. While the stories are typically extreme situations, viewers tend to connect to the people because, as flawed humans, we can all relate. Most of these shows have a "look back" section showing a time when life seemed normal, before everything spiraled down a dark path. At some point, trouble began, and you can easily see when the person started going off the rails. Yet, as we watch, we root for them to find a new way to live.

For *Dr. Phil*, at the start there seems to be no hope, but then breakthroughs really begin. Once the issue is discovered, a plan is crafted to deal with it. The common thread for these types of shows is getting to the real story. While Dr. Phil already knows the answer that will be revealed at the end, he never starts there. He first presents viewers with the conflict.

As a gospeler, that's my approach too. I don't jump to provide an answer without finding out about the person's life. There are usually some conflicts to discover first. In a conversation with folks like that young lady, I may not even lead with Jesus. Like those TV shows, people need to identify the problems in their lives before they will listen to a solution. Also, they may have some preconceived notions about Jesus or He may not matter to them in any way, at least not at first. So, I start with their story, because Jesus has a solution for *every* part of anyone's story.

Let's take a look at an encounter Jesus had with His disciples in John 14 where He was offering them God's hope for the future:

"Do not let your hearts be troubled.
You believe in God; believe also in me.
My Father's house has many rooms; if that
were not so, would I have told you that I am going
there to prepare a place for you? And if I go and
prepare a place for you, I will come back and take
you to be with me that you also may be where I am.
You know the way to the place where I am going."
Thomas said to him, "Lord, we don't know where
you are going, so how can we know the way?"

John 14:1-5

As I begin to share the Gospel with anyone, one of the first verses I read is verse 6:

Jesus answered,
"I am the way and the truth and the life.
No one comes to the Father
except through me."

On the TV shows I mentioned, they cover a lot of different problems and there may be a number of possible solutions, but when it comes to the nature of sin, there is only *one* answer for the cure. There's just one path to salvation. Just one person who can save and rescue any of us. Jesus alone is the Way, the Truth, and the Life, because of His death, burial, and resurrection.

So, what happened to the young lady who came into the First Step room? She came back another Sunday and talked to one of the ladies who was in the First Step room, telling her, "I'm just desperately looking for a community who could love me." And for the first time in her young life, she had found just that.

REFLECTION QUESTIONS

How might the examples of the way those TV shows deal with a major issue help you better understand how to approach someone with the Gospel?

Why do you suppose so many people today struggle with the idea that there is only one way to salvation, as Jesus said in John 14:6?

WHAT'S SO GOOD ABOUT THE GOOD NEWS?

We can start a conversation that leads to transformation.

For the past several years, I have traveled all over the U.S. speaking at all kinds of events. On a particular trip, driving to the airport, I saw a church marquee that said, "When did we lose the good part of the Good News?" That's one of those messages that, at first, you might laugh at the irony in the words. But then quickly you realize it's actually not very funny. Because it's true. Do we really believe the Good News is still *good* today?

One of the reasons why it might not seem as good is because we have become too focused on the bad news. As Christians, we seem to be putting a lot of time and energy into talking about all the darkness around us. Now, I get it. I totally agree that bad news seems to be louder than ever these days. But that's exactly why we have to keep reminding ourselves that we aren't called to tell everyone how dark the world is, but to keep talking about the Light. That also means we'll need to stop the infighting and arguing over trivial differences in our faith and disagreements about the Bible. We can refocus on pointing to Jesus and keeping Him our priority. Stop looking inward at our own problems and start reaching out with the answer.

I believe one of the best ways to hit refresh on the Good News is to remind ourselves how great it is. Throughout the book of Romans, the apostle Paul tells us that when we had no hope, when we had no answers, Jesus came to offer everything we need to be made right with God. Because the work has been done, now the message can be shared.

> *For everyone has sinned; we all fall short of God's glorious standard. Yet God, in his grace, freely makes us right in his sight. He did this through Christ Jesus when he freed us from the penalty for our sins. For God presented Jesus as the sacrifice for sin. People are made right with God when they believe that Jesus sacrificed his life, shedding his blood. This sacrifice shows that God was being fair when he held back and did not punish those who sinned in times past, for he was looking ahead and including them in what he would do in this present time. God did this to demonstrate his righteousness, for he himself is fair and just, and he makes sinners right in his sight when they believe in Jesus.*
>
> ROMANS 3:23-26 NLT

In just four verses, we get a lot of great news from the Good News! While everyone has sinned, God presented Jesus as the sacrifice that demonstrated His righteousness to set us right. While we have all fallen short, Jesus freed us from sin by His shed blood on the cross. What are we asked to do to receive all this? Believe in Jesus.

Now, truly believing in Jesus isn't just a casual agreement or mental understanding. It isn't a decision to try to live more of a morally upstanding life, all the while hoping to be blessed by God with things like money, security, and health. Believing in Jesus requires complete surrender. It's a total life change that causes us to begin walking in obedience to God as sold-out followers of Jesus. The problem is that we miss what we signed up for in the first place. Then no wonder so many folks aren't sharing the Gospel. In fact, not understanding what it means to *believe* could be why so many never even think about sharing.

In this moment, it doesn't really matter how you got here or what you may have done with your faith up to this point, because I want you to understand the Gospel and see how amazing His grace really is. I want you to grasp how following Jesus is best lived out by caring about people and wanting everyone to know that what you have received, they can receive too. We can start a conversation that leads to transformation, helping the lost be found, bringing those spiritually dead to new life, and yes, taking light into the darkness. We just need to stay focused on the message that, while there will constantly be bad news, the Good News of Jesus is always greater.

REFLECTION QUESTIONS

Why do you think so many people—Christians or not—are focused on all the bad news these days?

How can Romans 3:23-26 encourage you to keep the Good News your priority and begin to include it in your conversations?

THE LINE OF FAITH

What Jesus did is the only reason we can live the life that produces the fruit of the Spirit.

After I've heard someone's story and I'm sharing the Gospel, one of the main passages I always read is Galatians 5:19-24. In just six verses, Paul paints a very clear line between the two types of lives people can *live*. One is led by the Holy Spirit and the other is clearly not. We will see this line throughout the New Testament in terms like *light* and *darkness*, *dead* or *alive*, *lost* or *saved*. The more religious terms can be *flesh* vs. *Spirit*, *sin* and *salvation*, and *heavenly* or *worldly*.

When hearing someone's story, you may feel like you can pick up on which side of the line the person stands. But I never judge or make that call. I just read the Scriptures and let the Holy Spirit do the work. I highlight the word *live* in the passage because it's important and will always come up again later in the conversation. Here's the passage:

The acts of the flesh are obvious: sexual immorality, impurity and debauchery; idolatry and witchcraft; hatred, discord, jealousy, fits of rage, selfish ambition, dissensions, factions and envy; drunkenness, orgies, and the like. I warn you, as I did before, that those who live like this will not inherit the kingdom of God. But the fruit of the Spirit is love, joy, peace, forbearance, kindness, goodness, faithfulness, gentleness and self-control. Against such things there is no law. Those who belong to Christ Jesus have crucified the flesh with its passions and desires.

GALATIANS 5:19-24

That seems really clear, right? You either *live* like this or *live* like that. Usually, I ask the person point blank, "Does your life look more like the top list or the bottom? The flesh or the fruit?" This is the part of the conversation where you might feel uncomfortable, but Paul just comes out and writes, "those who *live* like this will not inherit the Kingdom of God." Keep in mind that you aren't saying this, Paul is. He had *lived* a very long time on the wrong side of that line before he met Jesus.

Thankfully, Paul doesn't say anyone who has ever committed one of these sins will not inherit the kingdom, but "those who *live* like this." Because Paul gives a very clear line here, I like to draw out an actual line and then ask, "Which side would you say you're on?"

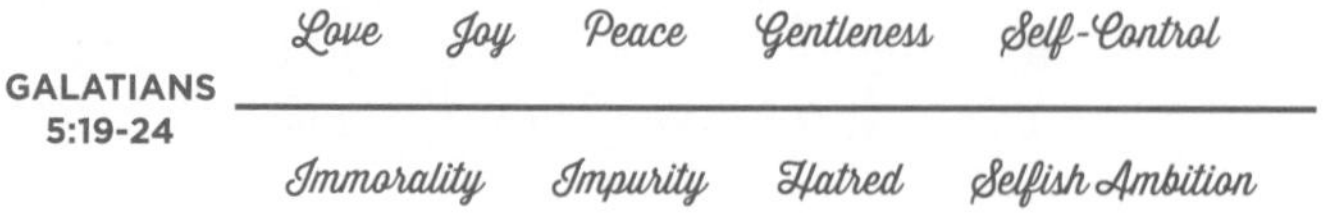

Love Joy Peace Gentleness Self-Control

GALATIANS 5:19-24

Immorality Impurity Hatred Selfish Ambition

Over the years, I have gotten all sorts of answers. Some say, "below the line, for sure," while others feel like they've "done enough good in life" to be on the fruit side. Some are not sure how they *live*, which is interesting. Like when the woman at the well told Jesus she didn't have a husband, that was partially true, but not the whole story. To try and get the complete picture, I may ask, "How do you think your friends or family would say you *live*?"

Paul starts by saying "the acts of the flesh are obvious." If the person isn't ready to be honest, then they also may not be ready to make a move towards Jesus. I'm not there to nitpick someone. I'm not there to argue or judge, but just ask the question, "Do you *live* like this or that?"

Most often, the person's story makes it very clear how they are living. For instance, I have talked to people who start the conversation with, "I just got a DWI last night" or "My wife kicked me out of the house" or "I have a problem. Can you help me?" I still read the passage and ask the question, but the answer is quite clear. There have also been times when, months later, the person comes back and reveals that they were not honest with me. That's why we have to let the Word and the Holy Spirit work to convict someone's heart. There's no need to try and figure out other people's lives for them.

For any of us, sin can certainly be hard to admit. We've all heard the saying, "To deal with a problem, you have to first admit you have a problem." We can't sugarcoat what we have to deal with. The woman at the well had to be honest about her past to begin to live differently. In fact, when she told the town, "He told me everything I have ever done," that seemed to be a positive, not a negative.

Many people I have talked to don't want to *keep living* the way they *are living. Living* the wrong way, they see the negative outcomes. The fallout of our sin is often the very thing that opens us up to Jesus in the first place. You can look at Paul's first list and see how they all lead to misery. If those were read in a wedding ceremony as the way one spouse wants to *live*, the ceremony would end quickly.

The second list is what Paul refers to as "the fruit of the Spirit." Now, that list certainly would make it into some marriage vows; a list you would want in a friend; a list you want your kids to *live* out. This is the fruit that should fall off our branches because of who *lives* in us. Just like apples fall off apple trees, the Holy Spirit will produce this fruit. For a visual, I will often draw a simple tree for people.

Those who belong to Jesus have stopped *living* like the first list and now *live* like the second list. When I draw the line, I put the sin on one side and the fruit on the other. I may write some of the things they mentioned in their story on one side of the line or the other for a visual to help them see where they are. None of us want to admit we are bad people, but how we are *living* is how we are *living*, period.

I have asked some people whether they thought they would go to Heaven or Hell. That can be a frightening question because it's easy to feel uncomfortable making that prediction. The idea is that if they say Hell, then surely they'll do whatever it takes to go to Heaven. The problem is they may say Heaven only because they don't like the alternative. They may even feel they have to do something to earn their spot. But, as I will soon make clear, it's nothing we do, but what Jesus did that is the only reason we can *live* the life that produces the fruit of the Spirit.

Being a gospeler, the line of faith can be hard to walk through with people. But it can be the very moment where folks realize their actions have separated them from God and they need help.

REFLECTION QUESTIONS

Why do you think Paul gave us such specific evidence to show the difference in "the acts of the flesh" versus the fruit of "those who belong to Jesus"?

How can having such a clear line to show someone help you as a gospeler?

FIRST THINGS FIRST

There has to be a first step before there can be next steps.

As we introduced yesterday, after walking through Galatians 5 and the line of faith, let's say the person you are talking to feels they have not been living the life like "those who belong to Jesus." What now? Well, we have to start the process of telling them how a new life can start. If the first step is admitting there is a problem, how can they fix it or who can fix it? Before I give them a list of things to start doing, I need to help them understand why anyone would want a list at all. This is the time to introduce Jesus—who He is and what He did for humanity.

Today, I want to talk about a passage from one of my favorite chapters in the Bible. I always read this when I share the Good News. Even though Paul was writing to the new believers in Corinth, I've found these verses can be great for someone who may not believe at all. They also work well when I talk to someone who is holding onto a lot of religion and may be distracted from who Jesus is and what the Gospel really means. Then there are the folks who have heard a preacher and raised their hand to his invitation, but never actually understood what they were committing to in that first step.

The truth is, if you don't *start* with Jesus, the Christian life just won't work. Nothing will be productive unless you are introduced to Him and understand what He did (and does) for you. You have to stay focused on Him, nothing else. One of the main reasons I like to read these verses is because they go straight to what is "of first importance."

> *Now, brothers and sisters, I want to remind you of the gospel I preached to you, which you received and on which you have taken your stand. By this gospel you are saved, if you hold firmly to the word I preached to you. Otherwise, you have believed in vain.*
>
> 1 Corinthians 15:1-2

In the first verse, Paul reminds us that we don't just "receive" the Gospel, but "take our stand" on the Gospel. Anytime we say that someone has taken a stand on something, we know that means business. That's no casual, flippant remark. Anyone who takes a stand on anything means he or she is serious and intentional. Taking your stand provides evidence that your belief is very real. Also, taking your stand is constant. There is no "I used to take a stand" or "I have in the past," because it's an ongoing action of taking a stand, not something you once did.

Let's move on to verses 3 and 4 where we find the key phrase I want to focus on:

> *For what I received I passed on to you as of first importance: that Christ died for our sins according to the Scriptures, that he was buried, that he was raised on the third day according to the Scriptures.*
>
> 1 Corinthians 15:3-4

While Paul was basically saying, "Hey! Don't miss this!" what does he say is "of first importance"? Church attendance? Good deeds? How many hours we pray? No, nothing we *do*, but what Christ has *done*. He died for our sins, was buried, and raised from the dead on the third day, just as He said He would do. That is the heart of the Gospel. Not worldly wisdom or religion, but the cross and the empty tomb. It really is that simple—exactly what baptism symbolizes—death and burial of the old and resurrection of the new person in Jesus.

Every time someone has shared their story with me, I've also heard what is "of first importance" to them. That's where you look for the Gospel, where you listen for evidence of what Paul said in Galatians 5, "those who belong to Christ Jesus." If someone tells me their life story and never mentions Jesus or what He did for them, that's an indication of what their whole life is about and not about. And, believe me, I have heard many stories where someone talks about a lot of religious things and never even mentions the name of Jesus.

My mom and dad held on tight to 1 Corinthians 15:1-4 all those years ago as they were committing to their new life in Christ. To this day, our whole family still uses these verses to lay the foundation for the most important thing in our lives—the Gospel, the Good News of Jesus Christ. So, let me ask: What is "of first importance" to *you*? That's a very important question to answer as we keep taking the steps toward becoming a gospeler.

REFLECTION QUESTIONS

Why should listening to a person's story let you know what is truly important in their life?

What was your answer to the question, "What is 'of first importance' to you?"

IF AND OTHERWISE

If we say we know Jesus, it's vital that our lives look very different than those we are trying to win over.

Let's stay in the flow from yesterday and talk more about 1 Corinthians 15 where Paul was making sure the disciples in Corinth didn't miss the real reason why they had committed to following Christ. With that focus, let's read those verses again.

Now, brothers and sisters, I want to
remind you of the gospel I preached to you,
which you received and on which you have
taken your stand. By this gospel you are saved,
if you hold firmly to the word I preached to you.
Otherwise, you have believed in vain.
For what I received I passed on to you as
of first importance: that Christ died for
our sins according to the Scriptures,
that he was buried, that he was raised
on the third day according to the Scriptures.

1 Corinthians 15:1-4

Yesterday, your first reflection question was, "Why should listening to a person's story let you know what is truly important in their life?" When you are getting to know someone, one of the first things you can pick up on is what is important to him or her. How? Because when something is a priority to us, we tend to talk more about that. If someone just can't seem to stop bringing up someone or something, everyone knows that it is a big deal in their life. This is also true in how you can tell if someone is in love—they can't stop thinking and talking about that other person. When I am talking to people about their life story, I listen for the Gospel. If someone can tell me their story and not mention Jesus, it tells me where they likely stand in a relationship with Him.

This is exactly why, first thing in a conversation, I want to listen and pick up on what's important to the person. I have no idea if they have received the Gospel or not and I don't want to make any assumptions about their faith. Because if I'm wrong, that could cost someone never hearing the Good News. Afterwards, I can share this Scripture passage that tells us what should be "of first importance" in all our lives if we are committed to Jesus. If I find out they have "received" it, the rest of the conversation can shift because we have something major in common. If the person hasn't, then I have much to share in explaining the Gospel.

The first subtitle the TV network came up with for *Duck Dynasty* was "Money, Family, Ducks." The first time I saw that phrase I knew right then that the network didn't know us very well. For one of our first public appearances, they had printed up thousands of cards for us to autograph with that line printed above our picture. Of course, we didn't want "money" being one our core descriptions because it's not. So, like Paul encouraged us to do in 1 Corinthians 15, we made a stand. Every single time we signed one of those cards, we drew an *X* through *money* and wrote *FAITH*. That actually drew more attention to the new word we wrote.

In verse 2 when Paul said, "if you hold firmly to the word I preached to you. Otherwise, you have believed in vain" there are two qualifiers, "if" and "otherwise," because a choice has to be made as we look at both sides. Paul knew that some of the people simply would never truly know Jesus. They might come in hot, but quickly flame out. But that's exactly why we must have these Gospel conversations. Many folks have heard about Jesus, yet over time, they didn't or won't "hold firmly" to what they were taught. Somehow, they miss Him.

When I'm listening to someone's story and he or she tells me about being saved and baptized at a camp or revival service as a kid, I always ask the question, "So, how's life been since then?" It's a fair question. Jesus charged us with making disciples, not with finding out if anyone has ever had a religious experience. If a person tells me they "got saved" at eight years old and then lived a dreadful life of sin ever since, I ask them if they think that sounds like how a disciple of Jesus lives. I don't question what happened at age eight, nor do I give them some sort of "religious pass" because they said "Jesus" once. That's between them and God. I'm just asking questions. When we make assumptions, we stop asking questions. That's why if we say we know Jesus, it's vital that our lives look very different than those we are trying to win over. Let's close today with the end of chapter 15:

"Death has been swallowed up in victory." "Where, O death, is your victory? Where, O death, is your sting?" The sting of death is sin, and the power of sin is the law. But thanks be to God! He gives us the victory through our Lord Jesus Christ. Therefore, my dear brothers and sisters, stand firm. Let nothing move you. Always give yourselves fully to the work of the Lord, because you know that your labor in the Lord is not in vain.

1 CORINTHIANS 15:54-58

Because death is inevitable, we need to start investing in what is *beyond* this life. The great news is that if someone's story doesn't reflect Jesus or, maybe has in the past but not in a long time, life can be turned around. Bury the old and let Jesus raise up the new. That's the *first step.* For us all, the *next step* is showing the world something real by letting Jesus live in and through us. Remember—His life can empower us to become bright lights in a dark world. That's of first importance.

REFLECTION QUESTIONS

How might someone think he or she has faith, but actually miss Jesus?

Why do you suppose Paul would strongly encourage believers to "hold firmly to the word I preached to you"?

SO, WHAT SHOULD WE DO?

We are the messengers, but the power of the message comes from the Holy Spirit.

On the Day of Pentecost in Acts 2, there were devout Jews from every nation gathered in Jerusalem. What perfect timing for the Holy Spirit to arrive, just like Jesus had promised would happen. But this event evidently didn't take place quietly. All these folks started hearing the disciples preach the Gospel in their native languages. The best analogy we might be able to understand is if a group of people suddenly started preaching at the Olympics where everyone there could hear about Jesus in their own language. So, how did the crowd respond to this miracle?

They were completely amazed. "How can this be?" they exclaimed. "These people are all from Galilee, and yet we hear them speaking in our own native languages! Here we are—Parthians, Medes, Elamites, people from Mesopotamia, Judea, Cappadocia, Pontus, the province of Asia, Phrygia, Pamphylia, Egypt, and the areas of Libya around Cyrene, visitors from Rome (both Jews and converts to Judaism), Cretans, and Arabs. And we all hear these people speaking in our own languages about the wonderful things God has done!" They stood there amazed and perplexed.

"What can this mean?" they asked each other.

ACTS 2:7-12 NLT

"How can this be?" and "What can this mean?" were two great questions asked after this sermon by Peter—the same disciple who had failed in answering his own three questions about Jesus during the trials. But, now, he was ready to take his stand on the Gospel. Peter had learned from his mistakes and wasn't going to shrink back and deny His Lord ever again. Filled with the Holy Spirit, he started preaching the very first post-ascension sermon, doing exactly what Jesus had told them to do.

But God knew what would happen,
and his prearranged plan was carried
out when Jesus was betrayed. With the help
of lawless Gentiles, you nailed him to a cross
and killed him. But God released him from
the horrors of death and raised him back to life,
for death could not keep him in its grip.

ACTS 2:23-24 NLT

Peter tells the crowd about Jesus' death and being raised from the dead, which will become a recurring theme among all the disciples. (That's why Paul said it is "of first importance.") Peter had seen everything take place with his own eyes and is now telling everyone.

Now, as someone who has shared the Gospel countless times, I can tell you first-hand that, after you have given the message about Jesus, the very best thing you can hear from a person is exactly the last question this group asked:

Peter's words pierced their hearts,
and they said to him and to the other apostles,
"Brothers, what should we do?"

ACTS 2:37 NLT

Peter may have been the messenger, but the power of the message that created this response was from the Holy Spirit. Remember what Jesus told Peter back in Matthew 16:17: "You are blessed, Simon son of John, because my Father in heaven has revealed this to you. You did not learn this from any human being," (NLT). That same dynamic was happening here. You always want the person with whom you are talking to eventually ask this same question, "What should I do?"

I always read this next passage to anyone I share with because this was the disciples' launch point after Jesus left the earth:

Peter replied, "Each of you must repent of your sins
and turn to God, and be baptized in the name of
Jesus Christ for the forgiveness of your sins. Then you
will receive the gift of the Holy Spirit. This promise
is to you, to your children, and to those far away—
all who have been called by the Lord our God."
Then Peter continued preaching for a
long time, strongly urging all his listeners,
"Save yourselves from this crooked generation!"

ACTS 2:38-40 NLT

There are a number of different topics to consider here. Peter brings up repentance, baptism, and the Holy Spirit. Repentance and baptism are where the Spirit begins producing fruit that can pour out of our lives. For the person you share with, these terms will likely need to be discussed more to be understood. Remember, never assume what a person knows.

So, what was the outcome of Peter's first sermon?

> *Those who believed what Peter said were baptized and added to the church that day—about 3,000 in all.*
>
> ACTS 2:41 NLT

Jesus' Great Commission was being carried out. Notice Peter didn't say they needed to start going to church. They were starting the church! While God gave him the opportunity to preach to thousands, you can start by telling this same message to one person. If you are a believer, you have the same Holy Spirit.

We should be encouraged that the person responsible for this huge harvest of people was Peter, an average, everyday, working class guy who experienced incredible victories and life-shaking failures. He was normal. He was human. But, through it all, his faith in and obedience to Jesus made the difference and created a life that still inspires and challenges us. Today, our calling is the same one that Jesus placed on Peter's life—to have conversations that can lead people to ask, "Okay, what should I do?"

REFLECTION QUESTIONS

Why do you think inviting someone to ask their spiritual questions is an important part in sharing the Gospel?

Like Peter in Acts 2, how can knowing that you can rely on the Holy Spirit to do His work help you as a gospeler?

THE ROOTS AND FRUIT OF REPENTANCE

Choices have to be made for change before the results can become noticeable.

Yesterday, we read from Acts 2 where Peter preached the Gospel and told the people that they needed to repent. Today, I want to focus on what repentance actually means. We have to make sure we understand this important dynamic, first, in our own lives and then, second, when we share the Gospel.

Over the years, I've talked to quite a few people who have no religious background and were never in church to hear words like *repentance*, much less understand what they mean. So, first, let's get on the same page with a simple definition. Repentance means to turn from sin, change our minds about our direction, and look only to Jesus to lead us forward. Often, the word is connected to the military term of "about-face," meaning in one step, turn around and walk the opposite way, in the other direction. When someone has only known living by the sinful nature, especially when they have been deep in darkness for many years, repentance can be very challenging. Like they say, "Old habits die hard."

When a person is known by certain actions and attitudes, change can also be tough for others to accept. For different reasons, people may not have the grace to accept someone has truly changed. Take my dad, for example.

When he received the Gospel, everyone knew Phil was going to have to do a major "about-face" from where he had been. For Dad to walk with Jesus and live a new life, there was a lot that he had to give up and get away from. He would have to put down roots in his new life of repentance. This same thing was true for the woman at the well, Jesus knew she would have to deal with the past first to get ready for a whole new life.

I like to use marriage as an analogy for repentance because it's the closest thing most people can relate to in understanding a commitment to Jesus. If a guy gets married, but then just keeps living like he is single, how long is that going to work? If he keeps doing the same things with the same people and not behaving like a married man, the relationship is surely doomed. For a marriage to succeed, a major priority shift needs to be made at the altar and beyond. There are plenty of verses that tell us how Jesus has the same expectation as a spouse, if not more. Look at what He said in Luke 14:33: "In the same way, those of you who do not give up everything you have cannot be my disciples." His expectations for His followers are very clear. We all know that a person is married or single. It's not possible to be both. Going back to our line of faith from Galatians 5, everyone is on one side or the other.

Next, let's look at what repentance should produce in our lives. This example is straight from something that I experienced. Across parts of the South, you can find the mayhaw tree that produces small red berries, great for making jams and jellies. A few years back, I transplanted a grove of mayhaws onto my property. Now, an important point about this story is that I had eaten jelly from the berries these trees produced the year before I moved them to my property. So, I knew they could produce fruit. I couldn't wait to go out and pick them again to make my own jelly for years to come.

After the trees were carefully dug out to protect the roots, transported, and replanted, they all looked like they survived our relocation. But something happened that I never considered. The first year, no fruit. Second year, no fruit. Today, seven years later, while my trees are very much alive, they have never produced any berries. I have a grove of mayhaws, but no mayhaw fruit!

In John 15:5, Jesus taught, "I am the vine; you are the branches. If you remain in me and I in you, you will bear much fruit; apart from me you can do nothing." I can't tell you why my trees won't produce any fruit, I just know they don't. Yet, if a branch isn't producing the kind of fruit that it should be, then it has somehow lost connection to the vine or the source. When someone repents and is "transplanted" into Jesus, so to speak, any fruit that grows and shows will be His doing. He said the evidence will be clear: With Him, "much fruit." Without Him, "nothing," no fruit.

This is another reason why I start with the "old life" side of Galatians 5. That list of sins clearly shows the types of actions and behavior from which we need to repent. When we begin a relationship with Jesus, there will always be the very first act of repentance—the "about face." From there, the process of repentance will happen again and again as we journey through the daily life change

Jesus brings. Going back to my marriage analogy, in my own relationship of thirty-plus years, I have had to repent many times as I got out of line as a husband. Peter walked with Jesus for three years and was all-in, but then he blew it by denying Him. Then after Jesus' resurrection, Peter repented and radically changed. Repentance is a part of salvation, but also an ongoing journey in transformation.

For us all, choices have to be made for repentance, for change, before the results can become noticeable. God's Spirit alive in us is responsible for our ability to transform. Through Him, our choice to repent produces deep roots and much fruit to help us be faithful gospelers.

REFLECTION QUESTIONS

Why do you suppose repentance is harder for some people? What factors can make it easier or tougher for someone to change?

How might accepting the truth of "apart from me you can do nothing" actually be freeing for us to bear the fruit of the Spirit?

THE DIFFERENCE MAKER

People may see our lives as believers and wonder how they could be a part.

For any of us to leave behind a sinful past, there is definitely a need for God's Spirit—the third Person of the Trinity—to help. In John 14:26, Jesus said, "But the Advocate, the Holy Spirit, whom the Father will send in my name, will teach you all things and will remind you of everything I have said to you." The Holy Spirit teaches and reminds us about Jesus, while also empowering us in our opportunities to witness for Him. The fact that the Holy Spirit is always with us, helping us and giving us words to speak, is a huge source of Gospel courage. The Spirit is always doing the "heavy lifting." You'll notice that several times, I have mentioned praying and listening to the Holy Spirit to guide both me and the person I'm talking with. Praying is a good reminder that the Spirit is working and it's not all on us.

When I'm talking to people about starting their journey with Jesus, I keep my explanations of the Holy Spirit simple. I let the person read and discover about the Spirit living in them. As we saw in Galatians 5, the whole idea is that when God lives in us, we will become different. Because we all understand that bad things reside in our hearts, we can also understand the concept of God's Spirit alive in us to produce good in our lives.

In John 3, Jesus had an interesting exchange with a member of the Jewish ruling council who was super religious. As we take a look at this late-night conversation, watch for Jesus talking about the Spirit:

> *Now there was a Pharisee, a man named Nicodemus who was a member of the Jewish ruling council. He came to Jesus at night and said, "Rabbi, we know that you are a teacher who has come from God. For no one could perform the signs you are doing if God were not with him." Jesus replied, "Very truly I tell you, no one can see the kingdom of God unless they are born again." "How can someone be born when they are old?" Nicodemus asked. "Surely they cannot enter a second time into their mother's womb to be born!" Jesus answered, "Very truly I tell you, no one can enter the kingdom of God unless they are born of water and the Spirit. Flesh gives birth to flesh, but the Spirit gives birth to spirit. You should not be surprised at my saying, 'You must be born again.' The wind blows wherever it pleases. You hear its sound, but you cannot tell where it comes from or where it is going. So it is with everyone born of the Spirit." "How can this be?" Nicodemus asked.*
>
> John 3:1-9

Remembering that the crucifixion and resurrection had not yet happened, Jesus is telling this guy that people will have to be reborn, saying that water and the Spirit will be the combination. While Nicodemus appears to believe that Jesus is from God, he is obviously confused by His words, just as we all would be. Nicodemus also has trouble seeing how he can become a part of it all. This is a good reminder for us that people may see our lives as believers and wonder how they could be a part. That's why we can't expect them to figure all this out on their own. Here, Jesus is such a great example and inspiration because, while being very honest, He is also patient with Nicodemus.

"You are Israel's teacher," said Jesus,
"and do you not understand these things?
Very truly I tell you, we speak of what we know,
and we testify to what we have seen, but still you
people do not accept our testimony. I have spoken to
you of earthly things and you do not believe; how
then will you believe if I speak of heavenly things?
No one has ever gone into heaven except the
one who came from heaven—the Son of Man.
Just as Moses lifted up the snake in the wilderness,
so the Son of Man must be lifted up, that everyone
who believes may have eternal life in him."

JOHN 3:10-15

Jesus tells Nicodemus about "heavenly things," beyond what he can see; that we all must be born again; that the old must die and be made new. Because Jesus had come to earth as fully God, yet also fully man, He too was going to suffer death and be made new. When we get to Jesus' death in John 19, we see Nicodemus show up with Joseph of Arimathea to take His body for burial. Does this mean Nicodemus became a follower of Jesus? Well, we can't know for sure, but here's the bottom line: The moment someone chooses to believe in Jesus, they receive this very important Helper in their lives—the Holy Spirit. And this Helper is the living presence of God. Once the Holy Spirit comes to live within a person, that's when the Christian life starts to make sense as the Spirit begins His work of guiding, teaching, and transforming.

REFLECTION QUESTIONS

Why do you suppose the Holy Spirit is so often misunderstood? What is your experience?

Regarding the statement, "People may see our lives as believers and wonder how they could be a part of this as well," how might this encourage you to have more grace and patience with those you talk to about Jesus?

REFLECTION OF THE RESURRECTION

A person's baptism should reflect re-enacting and following the example of what Jesus did through His death, burial, and resurrection.

Today, let's talk about baptism. The word "baptize" means to "dip or plunge in water." As we discussed before, Jesus included it as part of the Great Commission. After Peter preaches that first Gospel message in Acts 2, the rest of the book is full of stories of folks being baptized after hearing the Good News.

Let's start by taking a look at Acts 2:38 and Peter's command:

Peter replied, "Repent and be baptized, every one of you, in the name of Jesus Christ for the forgiveness of your sins. And you will receive the gift of the Holy Spirit."

Peter doesn't explain John's baptism or mention that John baptized Jesus, but he definitely ties baptism to responding to the Gospel. In answering the question of "What should we do?" he connects baptism to repentance, the forgiveness of sins, and the Holy Spirit. We see the results in verse 41: "Those who accepted his message were baptized, and about three thousand were added to their number that day." Baptism must have been important if it immediately followed Peter's preaching and the people's response.

This would be a good time to recap what I have told you about how I share with people. I take time to ...

- Care about people,
- Talk with people,
- Get their story,
- Try to help them determine if they have a relationship with Jesus,
- Discuss and deal with sin,
- Stress that the Gospel is the most important truth where answers can be found.

In Acts, we see that getting baptized is a common response of obedience after hearing the Gospel. Today, we have the luxury of having the entire Bible to read all the references to important topics like this. Unlike the folks in those days, we have the New Testament to help us understand exactly what baptism means. At this point in the conversation, I usually go from Acts 2 to Romans 6:1-4. Here, Paul explains baptism more in depth than Peter did in Acts. He starts with a question, "What shall we say, then? Shall we go on sinning so that grace may increase?" Some had decided if the grace of God covers all our sin, then let's go sin! To that, Paul replies, "By no means! We are those who have died to sin; how can we live in it any longer?" This comes full circle back to what we talked about in Galatians 5 and "those who live like this." Paul is continually explaining that *how* we live our lives should be a big deal to "those who belong to Jesus." Now, let's move on to verses 3 and 4:

> *Or don't you know that all of us who were baptized into Christ Jesus were baptized into his death? We were therefore buried with him through baptism into death in order that, just as Christ was raised from the dead through the glory of the Father, we too may live a new life.*

This is the same exact language Paul used to describe the Gospel in 1 Corinthians 15. Here, he explains in more detail the connection between baptism and the Gospel. When we read this passage with people, they can better understand how baptism is simply a reflection of Jesus' death, burial, and resurrection. We have to die, bury the old person, and be raised. Raised to what? A *new* life! A newness that reflects the fruit of the Spirit that now lives in us.

When people tell me about any decision they made for Jesus in the past, I often ask them, "So, how's the new life been?" Over the years, I have gotten a multitude of answers. The problem can often come when the way someone has lived since that decision has had little to no reflection of Jesus. While I never doubt that something happened to a person at that time, I try to help them understand that it may not have been a reenactment of the Gospel—no death to the old self, no burial, and no new life. Perhaps, a nod toward God, but not rebirth. Always keep in mind—it's the person's life, so it's their call. We're just messengers, the gospelers showing them the Scriptures.

To sum up the importance of today's verses, Paul explained that we can't and shouldn't keep sinning the way we once lived. Why? Because we died to our old life, just as Jesus died on the cross. We were buried, just like He was buried. We were raised, just as He was raised to a new life. That's exactly what a person's baptism should reflect—reenacting and following the example of what Jesus did. His death, burial, and resurrection are the key factors of the Gospel that we need to make clear to those who need to know Him.

REFLECTION QUESTIONS

What does Acts 2:38 tell us about the importance of baptism and how it fits into our Gospel story?

How do you think Romans 6:1-4 can help someone understand the power and priority of the Gospel?

DECLARE WITH THE MOUTH, BELIEVE WITH THE HEART

Declaring and believing is letting go of the control of our lives and giving it to Him.

When I'm walking someone through the Bible, after reading Romans 6, as we discussed yesterday, I flip over a few pages to Romans 10:9-10.

If you declare with your mouth, "Jesus is Lord," and believe in your heart that God raised him from the dead, you will be saved. For it is with your heart that you believe and are justified, and it is with your mouth that you profess your faith and are saved.

ROMANS 10:9-10

It's amazing how difficult we can make salvation and how easy it is for us to lose sight of the simplicity of the Gospel. If we're not careful, a subtle shift can take place in our churches where we declare that it's Jesus who saves us, but in reality, we lay out a list of rules and expectations that people have to follow if they want to be Christians. "Oh, you want to be saved? Well, then you have to *start* to do this and say that and pray this and read that and join here, and oh yeah, definitely *stop* doing all that other stuff. And that's it, you're saved!"

Some of those "starts and stops" may be great things, but we forgot one thing, the main thing—Jesus! We begin to move the power of salvation off of Jesus and onto us. We focus on actions, not on a Person. We all know people who act like they have to work themselves to death for their salvation. They always feel like they're one step away from Hell, never quite good enough, always messing up. Maybe you have struggled with that yourself?

As you share the Gospel with others, never lose sight that the Good News is not a list of rules to start following just so we can be better people and figure out how to save ourselves. It's Good News because Jesus gave up His life as payment for our sin, so we can be forgiven and saved by simply placing our faith in Him. This truth is so powerfully written in Ephesians 2:8-9:

For it is by grace you have been saved,
through faith—and this is not from yourselves,
it is the gift of God—not by works,
so that no one can boast.

Going back to Romans 10, Paul tells them to do two things: "declare with your mouth" and "believe in your heart." At that time, Paul was constantly speaking against the idea that our own obedience to the law could somehow make us righteous. The truth is, the only thing the law can do is show us where we've messed up, which we've all done. The law can't make any of us perfect. Trying to earn our salvation is a losing battle. Paul reminded the Roman church that no accomplishments were going to save them, only Jesus. All we have to do is believe that He is truly God, that He came to earth and overcame death, and then make Him the Lord of our lives by confessing our faith in Him.

There isn't a checklist to mark off to find salvation. Declaring and believing is letting go of the control of our lives and giving it to Him. When we declare that Jesus is Lord, that means Lord of *everything*. We are laying down our lives at the foot of the cross and trusting Him to guide us going forward. That's why in several of his letters, Paul called Christ, the head, and us, the body.

Belief in God and a confession of Jesus as Lord is usually where a move toward God starts. Not just a one-time event, but the launching pad for a new lifestyle to be lived. Once again, I'll use marriage as an analogy in our commitment to Jesus. A marriage is marked by some kind of official ceremony, whether at a courthouse in front of a judge or in a church with hundreds of guests. There is a license to be signed, rings to be exchanged, and vows to be declared to each other and before those in attendance. At a wedding, there is a confession of the mouth about the commitment to a new life where two are joined as one. The two declare to love and be faithful for all the days to come, through thick and thin, from that day until death. Yet, to truly be successful after the wedding, a marriage needs to be the "death of the old man and woman" to the single life and a "resurrection to a new life" together. The belief in what binds them together and the confession that they will no longer be two but one going forward is what grafts them and puts down roots in their new life together.

We can see those truths in Romans 10:9-10 in our

commitment to God. There has to be a moment when we believe in the depths of our being that what Jesus did was enough for us. And then we need to declare to Him that He is the Lord of our lives. This can't be forced, and it can't be faked. As you share with others and get to these verses, don't try to force a confession. And you sure don't want the person to fake one. The choice is between them and God, and they are making a decision that will affect their eternity. The commitment has to be authentic and, when it's real, you'll know it. And so will the person.

REFLECTION QUESTIONS

What rules and expectations do you think we sometimes add on to becoming a Christian?

How does Romans 10:9-10 bring better understanding of the powerful connection between the mouth and the heart?

STOP AND COUNT THE COST

A divided heart isn't strong enough to follow Him all the way to the cross.

Going back to Romans 10:9-10 that we talked about yesterday, as I have shared that passage about believing and confessing over the years, I've noticed this may be the one thing that people actually remember doing at some point in life. I have heard, "Hey, I think I said that once!" They remember praying a prayer and saying some words at some point as a child or teenager, but somehow seemed to miss what it's all about. They never took a step towards discipleship (maturing in Christ) and actually pursuing a relationship with Jesus.

By this point in sharing with others, we have read multiple verses and passages. Especially when someone has made that initial step towards Jesus, I always want to present as clear a picture of the Gospel as possible and explain what being a disciple of Jesus is all about. I would do an injustice to anyone I spoke to if I did not let them know as much as I could about the Christian life.

Jesus gave us a glimpse of what making Him the Lord of your life can look like. In Luke 14, at the height of His ministry with a large crowd gathered around, it seems like Jesus decided to push back on the people's motives for following Him. Let's start with one of the harshest, toughest, and, to some, most confusing statements He ever made.

Large crowds were traveling with Jesus, and turning to them he said: "If anyone comes to me and does not hate father and mother, wife and children, brothers and sisters—yes, even their own life—such a person cannot be my disciple. And whoever does not carry their cross and follow me cannot be my disciple."

LUKE 14:25-27

Can you imagine being in the crowd that day? Perhaps you had heard about Jesus, about His teaching and incredible miracles, so you leave your home and travel for days just to get a glimpse of Him. You stand in the hot sun for hours with thousands of others who have also left their homes to see Jesus, all wondering if He's the long-awaited Messiah. Notice that Jesus doesn't stop and say, "Wow, this thing is really growing! Be sure to come back next week and bring a friend." He didn't base His mission on what would grow the biggest crowds, and He wasn't about to start lowering the bar to keep them there. Jesus knew how difficult the path of discipleship was. He knew the kind of spiritual warfare and persecution His followers were going to face.

So, what does Jesus tell this enormous crowd? He tells them that if they're going to follow Him, they'll have to hate their families and even themselves. *Wait ... what?* Isn't Jesus all about love? How many folks do you think might have just started walking away right then? It's possible some people didn't even stick around to try and understand what He meant. But Jesus knew exactly what He was saying. If this thing was going to work, they were going to have to be *all in*. He was going to need their complete allegiance. Their love for Him would have to reign supreme. A divided heart isn't strong enough to follow Him all the way to the cross.

Jesus invites His followers to die to themselves and carry a cross as He was about to do. He was warning them that He was going to expect His disciples to practice what they professed about Him; to declare with their mouths and believe with their hearts as we talked about yesterday. He continued on this same theme with a story about someone who built a tower.

> *Suppose one of you wants to build a tower. Won't you first sit down and estimate the cost to see if you have enough money to complete it? For if you lay the foundation and are not able to finish it, everyone who sees it will ridicule you, saying, "This person began to build and wasn't able to finish."*
>
> LUKE 14:28-30

Wouldn't a person making such a public commitment as building a tower for everyone to see make sure the funds were there to finish before starting? After all, no one congratulates someone for having *almost* built a tower. The same is true for us. No one is going to praise you for building ninety percent of a house or writing half a book or starting a new exercise plan and then quickly giving up. And none of these tasks compares to what it means to be a disciple of Jesus. A wise person counts the cost of what it will take before ever starting in the first place. Before you lay down the first brick, before you take the first step, know that you can see the commitment through to the end.

Jesus ended this teaching with a powerful declaration: "In the same way, those of you who do not give up everything you have cannot be my disciples" (Luke 14:33). Jesus doesn't just ask for part of our lives; He asks for everything. He doesn't just want our Sundays; He wants the rest of the week too. The Gospel is too important to go halfway and give up.

Like I said at the beginning of today, many of the folks I talk to may remember saying Jesus would be their Lord at one time, but I'm not sure all of them understood what they were really committing to. As we go and share the Good News, the temptation is always there to water down the Gospel, to lower the bar enough so they'll easily say yes. That's not what Jesus did and it's not what we need to do either. We have to let people know the commitment it takes to become a true follower of Jesus and allow them to count the cost before moving forward.

REFLECTION QUESTIONS

What are your thoughts on this statement: "A divided heart isn't strong enough to follow Him all the way to the cross"?

Was there a point in your life that you made a commitment to Jesus but didn't really understand the commitment you had made?

THE DOUBLE-EDGED SWORD

If someone tells me they feel like they are right with God, I'm not going to argue or debate what they think.

On a deer hunting trip in the Midwest in the middle of winter, I met a guy named Jake. As we were driving to where we would hunt, I began getting his story. After walking him through many of the Scriptures I have shared with you, Jake was all-in. I ended up baptizing him in a shallow cow pond in freezing cold weather. After his salvation, Jake was fired up. He met with his brother who came to Jesus and was baptized too. Next, Jake wanted to get the Gospel to his father. He wanted his whole family to know the Good News he had found.

When Jake heard that I was going to be speaking at an event in Kansas City, he asked if I would talk with his father. Jake warned me that his dad was really rough-around-the-edges, and this would be a one-night, one-shot deal. When I got to the address Jake had given me, I saw that a few other guys were there. As usual, after I met his dad, I started asking questions to get his story.

Looking like he was in his early sixties, Jake's dad talked about a faith journey that started at the age of nine, to which I asked my go-to question, "Okay, so how's it been since then?" As he went on with his story, I could tell life had been rough. I also noticed he never mentioned anything about Jesus. His current life included regular one-night stands with women with the goal being to, in his words, "try them out and find another wife." His life was a mixture of Paul's list of sins in Galatians 5, and there was no doubt he was *living* that way. As I read more Scriptures to him, I could see he was trying to connect what happened to him as a kid with the self-centered life he had been living for decades since.

Now, if someone tells me they feel like they are right with God, I'm not going to argue or debate what they think. But, so many times, I have seen the Gospel move people in moments just like this. Still, I could sense he wasn't ready to go all-in like Jake and his brother had. He wasn't convincing me that he would give up his lifestyle, particularly pursuing women the way he was. In fact, I suspected he had dates set up for later that week. At this point in his life, he was no longer a naive nine-year-old kid, but a grown man who knew exactly what he was doing.

I had a strong feeling that truly changing and doing an about-face to repent was going to be a huge challenge for him. You could see the battle in his eyes and on his weathered face. He would have to make some big changes, ones that the people around him probably would not understand and would not be happy about. Having sat with many folks in situations like this, it seems it's very easy for them to second-guess the decision to change their lives, so it's important to be sure. It's so hard to know someone's heart in one meeting. Because I was not sure about him, like always, I didn't want to talk him into a decision. The person must deeply desire what Christ can do in their lives. There has to be that genuine "What must I do?" moment.

I decided to read him the passage we talked about yesterday—Luke 14:25-33—then I asked him point blank, "Are you going to give up this thing you're doing with women?" After pausing to think, to my surprise, he looked up at me and said, "Yes, I'm ready." So, after a little prep work, we all gathered around a small tub in the apartment bathroom, and I baptized him.

I could have made it all really quick in the beginning when he was saying the right things, but I was not going to make light of a huge decision. I knew I had to the let the Holy Spirit lead and the Bible do the talking. Just as the presence and help of the Holy Spirit give us courage to share the Gospel, God's Word is also a source of courage. The Word of God is powerful, and we must let it do its work.

For the word of God is alive and active.
Sharper than any double-edged sword,
it penetrates even to dividing soul
and spirit, joints and marrow; it judges
the thoughts and attitudes of the heart.

HEBREWS 4:12

That verse tells us that the Word judges, not us. Even Jesus didn't let everyone follow Him who said they were ready to join. In Mark 6:4-6 we're told that Jesus could not perform many miracles in His hometown because of their lack of faith. We can only do what we can do, and some people just don't want to change. But, for Jake, what started as a conversation on a hunting trip months earlier had led us to where, like so many stories in the book of Acts, he and his whole household had come to believe. Gospelers ask questions, share the Good News, and then get to have a front row seat to watch the family of God grow.

REFLECTION QUESTIONS

Why might someone who comes to Christ actually have the best opportunity to reach their immediate family?

How does the truth of Hebrews 4:12 help and encourage you as a gospeler?

THE LINE BETWEEN DARKNESS AND LIGHT

*No matter what we have done,
Jesus is our Advocate,
and His sacrifice is greater than all our sins.*

Today, I want to share the last passage I like to use when sharing the Gospel. While I have covered many Bible passages over the past three weeks, we have highlighted about six that I usually share with folks. Especially early in the conversation, I like to keep things simple, not too much information at one time. The person may have a lot going on in their minds and hearts, like opening up old wounds when talking about their story. Maybe there's a fear of consequences of the sin in their lives. They could be questioning what a new life could mean for them. Or they may have never even considered what Jesus has done for them. As I look at the Bible with them, I never want to lose sight of the main aspects of the Gospel.

First John 1 is a great chapter that starts with Jesus coming to earth and lays out why we should proclaim the Good News. In verses 1-4, John says that it actually makes his "joy complete" to share Jesus. I feel the same way when I share how good Jesus is with others. We don't share because of a checklist or out of guilt, but because we care and get true joy by passing on the Gospel. Our mission gives our lives meaning and purpose.

Here's 1 John 1:5–2:2:

> *This is the message we have heard from*
> *him and declare to you: God is light;*
> *in him there is no darkness at all. If we*
> *claim to have fellowship with him and yet walk*
> *in the darkness, we lie and do not live out the truth.*
> *But if we walk in the light, as he is in the light,*
> *we have fellowship with one another, and the*
> *blood of Jesus, his Son, purifies us from all sin.*
> *If we claim to be without sin, we deceive ourselves*
> *and the truth is not in us. If we confess our sins,*
> *he is faithful and just and will forgive us our*
> *sins and purify us from all unrighteousness.*
> *If we claim we have not sinned, we make him*
> *out to be a liar and his word is not in us.*
> *My dear children, I write this to you so that*
> *you will not sin. But if anybody does sin,*
> *we have an advocate with the Father—*
> *Jesus Christ, the Righteous One. He is the*
> *atoning sacrifice for our sins, and not only for*
> *ours but also for the sins of the whole world.*

This is great to share with someone as a validation of the journey you have been walking through. John establishes the two sides of the line of faith using words like *light* and *darkness*, *lies* and *truth*, and *deception* and *truth*. He also uses *walks* much like Paul uses *lives* in Galatians 5. That makes sense as we often interchange "our Christian life" with "our Christian walk."

John gives us encouragement as well as a warning. Verse 8 says we can't deny our sin, before or after salvation. He knew that as sinners we try to justify just about anything. We offer excuses such as, "My anger outburst was really his fault," "I only stole that because I really needed it," "I lied at work, but my job was on the line," "I was harsh with my kids, but they knew I was having a bad day," or "Yeah, I was prideful, but if I don't fight for myself, who will?"

Much like the line in Galatians 5, 1 John 1 lets people know they need to decide whether they are "walking in darkness" or "walking in the light." Verse 9 is the popular one-verse promise of everything Jesus will do when we confess our sin. Then chapter 2, verses 1-2 give us hope, reminding us that no matter what we have done, Jesus is our Advocate, and His sacrifice is greater than all our sins. If the person has decided to give their life to Jesus, have their sins wiped away by His grace, and start a new life, this helps them understand what to do when a sin occurs. An advocate speaks, pleads, or argues a case for someone else, so as our Advocate, Jesus goes before the Father on our behalf for our defense.

When we leave the old life behind, the blood of Jesus begins to pour over our new life making it clean. Once again, I think about marriage in this scenario. Even though I made a commitment decades ago, I haven't been perfect as a husband. I have had bad moments, bad days, and, let's be honest, sometimes even bad months. Even still, our union has lasted all these years and keeps growing stronger because of the commitment we made and the forgiveness we continue to give each other on those bad days. We are not perfect, only Jesus is perfect. And when we fail, He is there speaking to the Father for us.

When I wrap up sharing this passage and any discussion, I often ask the person, "Where do you think you are in all this?" Regardless of the answer you hear at that point, you can know that you have done a thorough job of letting the person know who Jesus Christ is and how to start following Him. You can let the Gospel do its work through the power of the Holy Spirit.

REFLECTION QUESTIONS

Have there been times in your life when you tried to deny or justify your sin? Are there issues in your life today that you need to be honest with God or others about?

What are some of the main differences between "walking in the light" and "walking in darkness"?

A PASSIONATE PLEA

When someone needs to make a decision for the Lord, mid-morning, mid-afternoon, or midnight, we have to be ready.

Once we have shared the Gospel and shown the two sides of the line of faith, it's time we let the person talk, so we can see what they have taken in. This may be the moment that God begins the work of revealing Himself to them and illuminating their hearts as they're thinking about eternity. We can't rush this process. If they need to think about it, let them think. If they need to go talk to other people first, by all means, encourage them to do that. They could have more questions, so we may have to keep studying. They may want to set up another time to continue the discussion. But always be prepared when the time is right and they decide to make a move.

While talking, it's okay to nudge them. With some folks, I have gotten really fired up for them to change their lives. There's a big difference between being passionate versus being pushy. Look at this powerful plea out of Peter's Gospel message:

With many other words he warned them;
and he pleaded with them,
"Save yourselves from this corrupt generation."

ACTS 2:40

He "warned" and "pleaded," showing that he was passionate about their lives! With the woman at the well, Jesus didn't accept her take on her marriage situation. He leaned in further. What was the response to Peter's plea? Acts 2:41 tells us, "Those who accepted his message were baptized, and about three thousand were added to their number that day."

Like we talked about in Day 21, that's why I didn't let Jake's dad off the hook as he talked about "trying out women." That attitude and those actions were so destructive, not just to him, but to all those women. He was deceiving himself because, so often, people walking in darkness don't know they're walking in darkness.

We have to remember the first part of Romans 6:23, not just the second half: "For the wages of sin is death, but the gift of God is eternal life in Christ Jesus our Lord." We can't just sit back and watch people destroy their lives with sin. At times, I have shared with a person some ways that I have let my own sin hurt me and my relationships. You may be talking to a person who is having risky sexual relationships, hooked on narcotics, stealing money from their employers, abusing their children or spouse, etc. These types of conversations aren't necessarily reflections of what they think about God, yet they are serious matters. Sharing about Jesus may be the last opportunity to save them spiritually, as well as physically.

You could be someone's last hope and that's why God has placed you in their path at that moment. There may be family and friends desperately hoping and praying that your conversation goes in the right direction. Remember, the trajectory of my own life was changed forever because a guy traveled to share this very same message with my father when Dad had no options left. He had lost his family, his job, and most everything. He needed to be warned, and he needed someone to plead with him to be saved from corruption, just as Peter said in Acts 2.

I had a pastor friend over to my house one night and he brought his friend, Charlie. Even though it had gotten late, I was talking about how I share the Gospel with people. Charlie listened as I went through Scripture verses and the common questions people ask me. Since he came with our pastor friend, I was not on "non-believer alert," but just sharing strategies on giving the Gospel.

When I finished, Charlie began to ask his own questions. That's when I got on alert! He had just recently started, in his words, "showing up to church." But he had never fully given his life to Christ and never been baptized. No one ever had a conversation with him about *his* relationship with Jesus, not even the pastor. So, on my back porch, Charlie declared, "I'm ready to do this ... now!"

Korie had gone inside, and as she came back out, I told her, "Go get some towels." She had heard me say those words before and knew exactly what it meant. Although she seemed a little confused as to who exactly was about to get in the water, I added, "Charlie is ready to reenact the Gospel through baptism." So, at around one in the morning, he and I waded into the pond by my house and did just that.

I shared this story because we never know when God

is going to drop someone in our path that needs to hear the Gospel. And, if we're not walking with the Lord ourselves, if we're not praying, studying His Word, and in daily fellowship with Him, we can miss the opportunity. It's so easy to get caught up in the minutia of our day-to-day lives that we stop thinking about eternity and miss the spiritual battles happening around us. We have to be ready when someone needs to make that decision for the Lord. Mid-morning, mid-afternoon, or midnight, we have to be ready. Sure, it can happen at a church service, but when it starts happening in other places on other days of the week, that's when it's time to look out for revival!

REFLECTION QUESTIONS

How can you develop a sharper spiritual focus to be ready to have life-changing conversations with others?

What practical steps do you need to take to be prepared to share the Gospel when God puts someone in your path?

EVEN IN THE MIDDLE OF THE NIGHT

In conversations with someone,
it's not about us, but about what
the Lord wants to do in the person's life.

In Acts 16, Paul and Silas were grabbed by a mob and dragged before the authorities who ordered them to be stripped, beaten, and thrown into prison. The jailer in charge placed them in an inner cell and put their feet into stocks. Even though Paul and Silas had to be in pain from the beating and the chains, at midnight, they were praying out loud and singing to God. Imagine that, wrongfully imprisoned and shackled, yet still praising God!

About midnight Paul and Silas were
praying and singing hymns to God,
and the other prisoners were listening to them.

ACTS 16:25

Did you catch that at the end? Others were listening to them. They were sharing the Gospel before they ever said a word to anyone else. Their actions alone spoke volumes. Never forget that people are watching you all the time. Many of us can do an injustice to our message by how we behave in front of others. When we act like a complete jerk in public or to our family, no one will want to hear what we have to say. These guys had a real reason to complain, but they didn't, and it paid off. What happened next was miraculous:

> *Suddenly there was such a violent earthquake that the foundations of the prison were shaken. At once all the prison doors flew open, and everyone's chains came loose. The jailer woke up, and when he saw the prison doors open, he drew his sword and was about to kill himself because he thought the prisoners had escaped. But Paul shouted, "Don't harm yourself! We are all here!"*
>
> ACTS 16:26-28

I'm going to be honest with you, I think if one of my buddies and I were in this same situation, I would have totally misread this miracle. I believe I would have assumed that God just miraculously provided a way out for us. I mean, think about it, the doors fly open, and the chains drop? I would have left the jail immediately! It would be easy to assume that, because I was faithful to God, He was making the situation right. And, after all the injustice this jailer carried out, didn't he deserve a terrible fate? I think most of us would have completely missed what Paul didn't—an opportunity to share. Somehow, he had the presence of mind to think, *This is not about me, but the jailer.*

Paul and Silas didn't run. They just saw another opportunity for the Gospel. Paul realized that this moment would matter. At the very time he could have left, he stayed. Paul knew that to be a gospeler, there is another step we have to take—to let people know *why* we act the way we do.

> *The jailer called for lights, rushed in and fell trembling before Paul and Silas. He then brought them out and asked, "Sirs, what must I do to be saved?" They replied, "Believe in the Lord Jesus, and you will be saved—you and your household." Then they spoke the word of the Lord to him and to all the others in his house.*
>
> ACTS 16:29-32

It's interesting that the jailer responded exactly like the people did to Peter's sermon in Acts 2, asking, "What must I do to be saved?" Paul's simple answer was "Believe in the Lord Jesus." However, Paul still doesn't leave. Wasn't that enough to say? "It's all about Jesus! Bye!" No. This is where we can, too often, fall short. We may say a few words about Jesus, but not take the time to actually speak the truth and read the Word with people. The goal isn't just knowledge; it's transformation. For Paul and Silas, everything else stopped because getting the Gospel to the jailer and his entire family was the goal: "Then they spoke the word of the Lord to him and to all the others in his house." Paul and Silas *lived* on mission, and with a guy right in front of them asking questions, they are going to *stay* on mission.

I believe another reason why Paul stopped and took the time for this man was because he remembered what his life was like before he met Jesus while on the road to Damascus. I'm sure that experiencing the isolation and blindness for several days often caused him to stop and reflect on the importance of deciding to live every moment of every day for the Lord. He was not going to let this chance go by without giving this man the same opportunity that Jesus had given him. Watch what happened next:

> *At that hour of the night the jailer took them and washed their wounds; then immediately he and all his household were baptized. The jailer brought them into his house and set a meal before them; he was filled with joy because he had come to believe in God—he and his whole household.*
>
> ACTS 16:33-34

Stories like this throughout the book of Acts should constantly remind and inspire us that when we're in random conversations with someone, wherever that may be, whenever that may be, it's not about us, but about what the Lord wants to do in the person's life. Just like I mentioned yesterday, at noon or midnight, on Monday morning or Saturday night and any time in between, these stories can happen all throughout your week too. The opportunities are already there, and God is ready to show you. You just have to start the conversation and follow the Spirit's lead. Don't just say Jesus is the reason or offer a quick prayer. Point them to the truth, stick around when they need help, and stay as long as it takes to win them over with the Gospel.

REFLECTION QUESTIONS

Take a moment to contrast the difference in looking at this jailbreak story through the lens of human nature versus seeing the circumstance through the eyes of faith.

Has there been any situation in your life where you realized God had something totally different planned than what it originally appeared to be? Explain.

IT IS WRITTEN

The Bible is our best example of folks writing things down to pass on.

When it comes to learning and understanding, Korie is a reader, which means she's also a "read the directions" person. However, I am not a great reader, but I love listening or watching. When we buy something that has to be put together, I'm the one studying the picture on the box, while she is reading the directions—proof that we definitely have different brains.

That said, when I'm sharing the Gospel, I always try to write down what I'm sharing with people. "Put it on paper!" is a phrase I have said more times than I can count, mostly in the business world. What I mean is, "We have talked a bunch, but now write it all down so I can go over it thoroughly and we are all clear on the details." Writing something down adds clarity and weight to any matter. That's also a good reminder to not put negative thoughts in writing and send them to someone. Hearing bad news is one thing, but when it's in writing we can read it over and over again, which can affect us so much more by getting stuck in our head.

Not only does writing down key parts of a Gospel conversation add clarity, but then the person can go back and review it again. I have used whiteboards many times, but, most often, all I have is just a sheet of paper. That has proven to be useful, because by the end, we have a record of everything we talked about. When we're done, I give them the paper to keep and look at later. When it's a whiteboard, thanks to our phones, they can snap a photo. This doesn't just help with their own spiritual growth, but if a spouse, friend, or parent asks them questions later, they have something to refer back to.

The Bible is our best example of folks writing things down to pass on. All the people who God inspired to write His Word proved incredibly valuable over thousands of years. Perhaps one of the most powerful moments of writing something down was when Jesus Himself wrote in the dirt. Powerful because it saved someone's life, not just spiritually, but literally.

At the beginning of John 8, Jesus was in the temple courts teaching when some religious leaders brought in a woman who had been caught in adultery. Under their laws, this was a capital offense calling for her immediate death by stoning. (It's interesting that the guy she was caught with doesn't show up in the story.) The mob of men surrounding the woman was ready to be her judge, jury, and executioner. But Jesus did the most unusual thing; he knelt down and began to write in the dirt. Not once, but twice. The Bible doesn't tell us exactly what He wrote, but one thing is obvious—it worked.

But Jesus bent down and started to
write on the ground with his finger.
When they kept on questioning him,
he straightened up and said to them,
"Let any one of you who is without sin be

the first to throw a stone at her." Again he stooped down and wrote on the ground.

JOHN 8:6-8

Like I said back on Day 12, I always start by drawing a line—the line of faith. As the person begins sharing, I'll highlight key parts of their story by jotting them down on paper. Here's an example of how that can look:

MY STORY...

Prayed a prayer and baptized at 8

Addiction to drugs for 8 years

Mom died when I was 22

Deal with Anxiety

Marriage is struggling

Wouldn't say God is an active part of my life

You can see in the above example, once it's written in front of them, it has weight. It's clear. It's their life based on a mixture of circumstances, things that were done to them, and their own choices.

Once you've heard their story and written certain parts down, you can begin walking them through the Scripture passages we have covered up to this point. As I share and we read the stories in the Bible together, I add them to the sheet of paper, staying focused on the line of faith. I make sure to highlight important words and ideas that we read, like death to life, darkness and light, believe, confess, repentance, and baptism. Once I'm done, the sheet may look something like this:

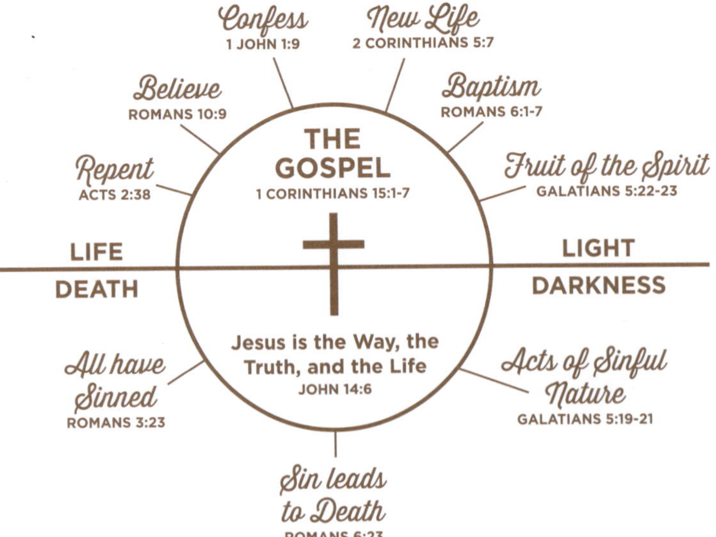

I want to encourage you to be specific as you share. Prepare yourself by learning the Scriptures we have discussed so far (from the graphic above), while also trusting that God will give you the right words to say in those encounters. Be bold to declare the Word of God and write it out for the person to leave no question as to who Jesus is and how they can move from darkness to light—from the life lived below the line to the life Jesus offers above the line.

REFLECTION QUESTIONS

Take a few minutes to look over the example I gave you of what I like to write down when sharing the Gospel. Consider what part you are comfortable with. What part might be intimidating?

What do you need to better understand to be ready to draw out the line of faith when given the opportunity to talk with someone?

SHARING YOUR STORY

No one can argue or debate a changed life.

In John 9, there is a multi-layered story about Jesus healing a man after the disciples start to ask Him questions about the connection between suffering and sin.

> *As Jesus was walking along, he saw a man who had been blind from birth. "Rabbi," his disciples asked him, "why was this man born blind? Was it because of his own sins or his parents' sins?" "It was not because of his sins or his parents' sins," Jesus answered. "This happened so the power of God could be seen in him."*
>
> JOHN 9:1-3 NLT

Next, Jesus bends down and makes some mud. Now, I grew up on the Ouachita River in Louisiana, so after a good rain, playing in the mud and having mud fights was something my brothers and I did a lot. But what Jesus did next was one of the most interesting and strange things in His entire ministry.

> *Then he spit on the ground, made mud with the saliva, and spread the mud over the blind man's eyes. He told him, "Go wash yourself in the pool of Siloam."*
>
> JOHN 9:6-7 NLT

Basically, Jesus took His spit and some dirt, made some mud, smeared it on the guy's eyes, and then told him to go wash it off. I'm sure people who were watching this thought Jesus was nuts! But everyone quickly forgot about the mud and spit after this:

So the man went and washed
and came back seeing!

JOHN 9:7 NLT

Some of the man's neighbors were so confused about him being able to see that they began to question if it was actually him. When the guy insisted who he was, he got sent to the "religious principal's office"—also known as the Pharisees. When they asked him what happened, the man just told the practical truth: "He put the mud over my eyes, and when I washed it away, I could see!" As usual, the Pharisees began to challenge Jesus and even question the man's miracle. Eventually, they even brought the guy's parents into the argument. Until, finally, he had enough.

So for the second time they called in the man
who had been blind and told him,
"God should get the glory for this, because
we know this man Jesus is a sinner."
"I don't know whether he is a sinner,"
the man replied. "But I know this:
I was blind, and now I can see!"

JOHN 9:24-25 NLT

After all the questions, confusion, debate, and challenges, the bottom line for this man came down to one simple fact: "All I know is because of Jesus, I was blind and now I see!" In every generation, there are going to be the haters and debaters who want to discredit, disprove, and discard the truth about Jesus. Those folks give us a very small taste of the kind of rejection that Jesus told us we would experience when we follow Him.

Yet, like the healed blind man, no one can argue with a changed life. Living proof, standing right in front of you, is hard to explain away. A great moment for any believer is when he or she gets to ask someone about their faith. But an even more amazing opportunity is when someone asks what has happened in your life because they see a difference in you.

REFLECTION QUESTIONS

Today is intentionally shorter to allow time for an important exercise. In place of questions, I want to encourage you to complete these four open-ended sentences to create a concise version of your Jesus story:

My life before Jesus was ...

I came to know Jesus by/through ...

My relationship with Jesus changed my life by ...

____

____

____

____

____

____

Today, God is at work in my life by/through ...

____

____

____

____

____

____

____

After you write out your story, go over it and memorize it to be able to tell others what Jesus has done for you.

WHO DO YOU THINK YOU ARE?

If you've believed the lie that you can't speak up, you may have forgotten who is living in you.

After Jesus' resurrection and ascension, we see in the book of Acts, chapters one through three, that everything seemed to be going great for the disciples. Thousands of people were coming to Jesus. Chapter four is where we first start to see some opposition rise up. The religious leaders didn't like Peter and John's message, so they arrested and threw them in jail. The next day, they brought the two disciples before the council in Jerusalem and asked them to explain the authority by which they were healing and preaching.

Then Peter, filled with the Holy Spirit, said to them: "Rulers and elders of the people! If we are being called to account today for an act of kindness shown to a man who was lame and are being asked how he was healed, then know this, you and all the people of Israel: It is by the name of Jesus Christ of Nazareth, whom you crucified but whom God raised from the dead, that this man stands before you healed. Jesus is 'the stone you builders rejected, which has become the cornerstone.' Salvation is found in no one else,

for there is no other name under heaven
given to mankind by which we must be saved."

ACTS 4:8-12

We can learn a lot from Peter's answer about how to concisely and effectively share the Gospel. The *only* authority they were operating under was made very clear: Jesus Christ. Verse 12 is so straightforward and unapologetic that the words have been repeated countless times over the centuries. So, how did the leaders respond to their claims? I love what verse 13 says:

When they saw the courage of Peter
and John and realized that they were
unschooled, ordinary men, they were
astonished and they took note that
these men had been with Jesus.

Many Christians today tend to think that only the highly educated or seminary trained folks can or should talk about Jesus. In our minds we think of Peter and John as these all-knowing, wise, foundational leaders and speakers for the global Kingdom of God. But that's not at all how they were viewed in their community. In fact, the whole reason all this was so confusing to the religious leaders was that these guys appeared to be nothing special. They were "unschooled, ordinary men," yet they were bold and courageous. Had Peter and John believed how their peers viewed them, perhaps they would have just kept quiet. Instead, they were filled with courage—

Gospel courage—that enabled them to speak clearly and powerfully about Jesus.

If you have believed the lie that you can't speak up because you have no training or a lack of knowledge, you may have never really understood or forgotten how powerful your God is and Who is living in you. As we clearly see in this story, Peter and John sure didn't let anything hold them back. They were fired up about the Gospel! In every generation, when someone is really excited about something or someone, people are going to take notice, especially at a time like today when so many are desperately searching for hope and answers.

After deliberation, the leaders decided to let Peter and John off with a warning to not speak or teach in Jesus' name anymore. So, how do you think that went?

But Peter and John replied, "Which is right in God's eyes: to listen to you, or to him? You be the judges! As for us, we cannot help speaking about what we have seen and heard."

ACTS 4:19-20

Here's a tough question: What if you started being a gospeler and someone in authority came and told you to stop? What would be your next step? Would you respond like Peter and John? When the two disciples told the other followers about the threat to shut down the Gospel, here's what they prayed:

"Now, Lord, consider their threats and enable your servants to speak your word with great boldness. Stretch out your hand to heal and perform signs and wonders through the name of your holy servant Jesus." After they prayed, the place where they were meeting was shaken. And they were all filled with the Holy Spirit and spoke the word of God boldly.

ACTS 4:29-31

There were no prayers of "Dear Jesus, keep us safe" or "Please send us where there are no threats to the Gospel." No, they actually prayed for *more* boldness! God obviously answered, because the church grew stronger and stronger, building a tight-knit community of folks who had each other's backs anytime, all the time. Sounds pretty great, doesn't it? In that day, fear and intimidation never stopped the Gospel. Even when Jesus' followers were arrested, beaten, and put in jail, the Good News just kept spreading. And, here we are, still talking about them, proving that their sacrifices mattered to our lives today.

How about you? Are you someone who "cannot help speaking about what you have seen and heard"? As gospelers, we need to allow these stories of the early disciples in the book of Acts to be our standard, not the folks around us today. We need to pray for boldness and courage in the power of the Holy Spirit to share the Gospel. Today, God is calling you and me to be like Peter and John—ordinary, unschooled folks who people can tell have been with Jesus and won't stop telling everyone what we have seen and heard about Him!

REFLECTION QUESTIONS

Why do you suppose Peter and John's boldness can seem so foreign to us today?

What is one situation in your life where you know God wants you to be bold for Him?

ASK THE QUESTION ANYWAY

What if just one person you led to Jesus brought thousands to Him?

Today, I want to share one of my favorite stories in the book of Acts that combines so many of the elements we've talked about in these pages—the Holy Spirit, being prepared, getting out of our comfort zones, telling others about the Gospel, and living on mission. This story involves Philip who came on the scene earlier in Acts 6. Philip was chosen to be part of a group of seven men who had a mission to serve and share the Gospel. And, boy, did they ever. After the apostles laid hands on them and prayed, we are told that the word of God spread rapidly (Acts 6:7).

The first to be individually highlighted in this group of seven is Stephen in Acts 7. (If you don't know the story, read it.) It is fascinating how gifted a gospeler he was, basically preaching the entire Old Testament in one lesson and pointing it all to Jesus! We can see clearly why he was chosen to be part of that group.

Tragically, after Stephen was stoned for his bold faith, in Acts 8 we read how the followers "scattered throughout Judea and Samaria" in the face of persecution. So, would this movement called *the church* fall off the tracks before it even got started? No. The story in Acts carries on with the next one of the seven mentioned, Philip. He was also a gospeler, ready to share the Good News with anyone.

Now an angel of the Lord said to Philip, "Go south to the road—the desert road—that goes down from Jerusalem to Gaza." So he started out, and on his way he met an Ethiopian eunuch, an important official in charge of all the treasury of the Kandake (which means "queen of the Ethiopians"). This man had gone to Jerusalem to worship, and on his way home was sitting in his chariot reading the Book of Isaiah the prophet. The Spirit told Philip, "Go to that chariot and stay near it." Then Philip ran up to the chariot and heard the man reading Isaiah the prophet. "Do you understand what you are reading?" Philip asked. "How can I," he said, "unless someone explains it to me?" So he invited Philip to come up and sit with him.

ACTS 8:26-31

First, notice that Philip was listening to the Holy Spirit and was obedient to do what he was told. If the Spirit led him to a stranger in a chariot, then he went. That kind of faith can certainly go against our human nature, right? Philip knew that his friend Stephen had just been killed for talking about his faith. But the seven and all the disciples were determined to get the message out to people who needed it.

The eunuch asked Philip, "Tell me, please, who is the prophet talking about, himself or someone else?" Then Philip began with that very passage of Scripture and told him the good news about Jesus.

ACTS 8:34-35

The eunuch was reading a passage from Isaiah 53 where the prophet prophesied about a Suffering Servant. Notice how Philip was prepared by not only knowing the passage, but also exactly who Isaiah was talking about. Here is the curious part of this story to me. The man had been worshiping in Jerusalem and is now reading the book of Isaiah on his way back to Ethiopia. This was a long journey, so he had lots of time to read. When Philip saw him, the eunuch was doing the things God's people typically do. I probably would have assumed the Spirit missed it on this one, telling him, "Hey brother, keep up the good work," and then go back to regroup with the others. But Philip did what good gospelers do, he simply asked a question, "Do you understand what you are reading?" *Brilliant!*

Philip did not let the appearance of godliness stop him from asking questions and giving explanations about Jesus. Our first question tends to be, "Do you go to church?" If we hear a no, we may invite them. If yes, we usually stop asking questions. Philip's method is way more productive, because going to a church doesn't make you a disciple of Jesus. That usually means you sit in a building for an hour or two a week to worship, pray, and listen to a sermon. I have seen many people come to the Lord who had a church they called home. Like Philip, we have to always ask questions, no matter how someone might appear to us.

> *As they traveled along the road, they came to some water and the eunuch said, "Look, here is water.*

What can stand in the way of my being baptized?" And he gave orders to stop the chariot. Then both Philip and the eunuch went down into the water and Philip baptized him.

ACTS 8:36-38

This shows us why we have to be prepared for moments like these. The eunuch was ready, right then and there. Philip could have just told him to go back home and celebrate his baptism with his family and friends. That way, they could invite grandma and grandpa and have a party. But, throughout the book of Acts, in these moments when people move towards Jesus, they went all the way. Not some quick little nod, but a "stop everything and let's get it done."

A while back, I did some research and came across a really interesting fact. Today in Ethiopia, 63 percent of the 113 million people there claim to be believers in Jesus Christ. I believe that's a majority in anyone's book. Here's a quote from an article in a 2019 edition of *Smithsonian* magazine, "In the dusty highlands of northern Ethiopia, a team of archaeologists recently uncovered the oldest known Christian church in sub-Saharan Africa, a find that sheds new light on one of the Old World's most enigmatic kingdoms—and its surprisingly early conversion to Christianity."

Is it possible that the very reason the Holy Spirit had Philip leave the crowds in Samaria to go talk to this one Ethiopian is because when the eunuch would return home, he would become the catalyst to influence and evangelize his entire nation? What if the Holy Spirit tells you to go to one person and that one ends up bringing thousands to Jesus? Like my aunt Jan told Pastor Bill when she stated, "If you convert Phil Robertson, he will convert a thousand!" We may never know until Heaven who or how many we affected and influenced by sharing Jesus.

REFLECTION QUESTIONS

Have you ever felt like you were supposed to talk to someone who, on the surface, appeared to already know Jesus?

____

____

____

____

____

What can you learn from Philip and the Ethiopian eunuch's story for your own journey of being a gospeler?

____

____

____

____

____

LOOKING BACK TO GO FORWARD

*From the very beginning,
God was preparing the
way for Jesus to come.*

Yesterday, we looked at Philip and the eunuch in Acts 8. Today, I want to dig a little deeper into how that interaction started. The eunuch was reading Scripture, but there was one problem. He didn't really understand what it was talking about. After the eunuch read the passage from Isaiah 53, the next verse says:

> *Then Philip began with that very passage of Scripture and told him the good news about Jesus.*
>
> ACTS 8:35

Two things stand out to me about how Philip was prepared to have a conversation with the eunuch. First of all, he knew about the book of Isaiah. When the eunuch asked who Isaiah was talking about, what if Philip had responded, "Man, I've never read that! I don't know. Maybe you should go ask a priest." But Philip didn't respond like that at all. He had read Isaiah, likely many times. He was very familiar with what the eunuch was reading. But even more than the fact that Philip was prepared, the main thing that stands out is how he responded. He knew that specific Old Testament prophecy pointed to Jesus.

Philip wasn't the first one to see that in Isaiah's prophecy. Not only did Matthew and John quote Isaiah 53 in their Gospels referring to Jesus (Matthew 8:17; John 12:38), but Jesus Himself quoted from the passage in talking about His own crucifixion (Luke 22:37). What if Philip didn't see how it pointed to Jesus? What if he missed it? He could have been familiar with the passage but still have no clue who this Suffering Servant was. He might have said, "That book is over seven hundred years old. I don't know who he's talking about."

We can sometimes treat the Bible that same way, especially the Old Testament. We find it hard to understand or to see how it relates to what we're going through today. So, we either avoid reading it altogether or we read but miss what it's really about. We see it as just some story or psalm or prophecy from thousands of years ago. We don't realize that it's all part of God's perfect plan. From the very beginning, God was preparing the way for Jesus to come.

The disciples didn't seem to get it at first either. You know how many times one of them quoted the Old Testament in the Gospels? Not once! But then something changed after the Resurrection. They finally saw the big picture, realizing that Jesus had just fulfilled the prophecies they had read so many times. Right off the bat in Acts 1, Peter quotes from Psalms as he talks about replacing Judas. Peter realizes that Jesus' life and death and resurrection didn't catch God by surprise. This was not some Plan B, but God's original plan all along.

In Peter's sermon in Acts 2, he quotes prophecies

from Joel and Psalms to show that Jesus was both Lord and Christ. In verse 23, he said it all happened through "God's deliberate plan and foreknowledge." He continues in the very next chapter, quoting from Genesis and Deuteronomy to show that Jesus had fulfilled the promises of the Old Testament.

Indeed, beginning with Samuel, all the prophets who have spoken have foretold these days.

ACTS 3:24

Peter wasn't the only one. Philip realized the same thing and was prepared to share it with the Ethiopian eunuch. James stood up at an assembly in Acts 15 and quoted a prophecy from the book of Amos. Paul regularly referenced the Old Testament in his letters. This encourages me that I don't have to become an Old Testament scholar, but I don't have to be afraid of it either. The apostles realized something that we can stand firm on today—God's plans are perfect. He's never caught off-guard. Even when things might look bad, He is in control. The Gospel has been God's plan from the beginning and has the same power to save people today.

REFLECTION QUESTIONS

Why do you think God has so many connections in the New Testament to the Old Testament, particularly in pointing to Jesus?

What are some practical steps you can take to knowing more of God's Word—Old and New Testament—for your own growth and to share with others?

THREE STRIKES AND A GRAND SLAM

Not only did Jesus forgive and restore Peter, but He gave him a mission for the rest of his life.

Today, I want to swing back to Peter and his complicated relationship with Jesus. I often think of all the amazing, bold Kingdom-building Peter did that we read about in the book of Acts. He was a rock, as Jesus called him, and a foundational pillar in Christianity. As for me, I don't think of him as the guy who messed up so badly by abandoning Jesus at His worst moment in life, likely because I know Peter was able to move on from his past and become the man God had in store for him to be.

Considering Peter's radical change from his cowardly denial of Jesus before the crucifixion to his bold leadership in the book of Acts, here are a few questions for you:

- Is there anything in your past that still has you convinced you don't need to talk to anyone about Jesus?
- Do you ever feel if people found out everything about you, they would ask why you think you can talk about God?
- Are you walking through something difficult right now and feel like there's no way you could ever speak to anyone about Christ's love and forgiveness?

- Are you feeling disqualified or unworthy and believe it's best to just keep your mouth shut?
- Have you ever shared the Gospel with someone who told you they couldn't say yes because they felt too shameful and guilty?

In some of Jesus' final moments with His disciples which we read about in Matthew 26:31-35, He told them that they would soon desert him. To no surprise, Peter boldly announced that, even if the other guys abandoned Jesus, he never would. That's when Jesus gave him the infamous prediction that, in just a few hours, Peter would deny Him, not once, not twice, but three times. Of course, in the moment, Peter couldn't see how that was possible, vowing it would never happen, even if he had to die trying. But, as always, Jesus was right:

> *Now Peter was sitting out in the courtyard, and a servant girl came to him. "You also were with Jesus of Galilee," she said. But he denied it before them all. "I don't know what you're talking about," he said.*
>
> MATTHEW 26:69-70

A girl's accusation. A public denial. Strike one.

> *Then he went out to the gateway, where another servant girl saw him and said to the people there, "This fellow was with Jesus of Nazareth." He denied it again, with an oath: "I don't know the man!"*
>
> MATTHEW 26:71-72

A different girl. (Notice these accusations didn't come from some person of authority like a Roman soldier, high priest, or government leader.) Yet another public denial, but this time, Peter went from a lie to a full-on disowning of Jesus with an oath. Strike two.

After a little while, those standing there went up to Peter and said, "Surely you are one of them; your accent gives you away." Then he began to call down curses, and he swore to them, "I don't know the man!"

MATTHEW 26:73-74

A crowd recognized Peter and confronted him. With his responses digging a deeper hole each time, he combined lying and denial with a curse upon himself. Strike three.

Immediately a rooster crowed. Then Peter remembered the word Jesus had spoken: "Before the rooster crows, you will disown me three times." And he went outside and wept bitterly.

MATTHEW 26:74-75

At that point, Peter likely thought his life with Jesus was over. He had done the very thing he vowed he would never do. He not only didn't speak up, but he tried to save his own butt at all costs. We all know the pain of a bad decision like this, don't we? Like Peter, in those moments, we can feel disqualified and worthless.

The next time we read about Peter is in John 21. What

was he doing? The only thing he knew to do. Fishing. Back to the very place where Jesus had found him. But watch for what sounds familiar in this next story.

> *"I'm going out to fish," Simon Peter told them, and they said, "We'll go with you." So they went out and got into the boat, but that night they caught nothing. Early in the morning, Jesus stood on the shore, but the disciples did not realize that it was Jesus. He called out to them, "Friends, haven't you any fish?" "No," they answered. He said, "Throw your net on the right side of the boat and you will find some." When they did, they were unable to haul the net in because of the large number of fish.*
>
> JOHN 21:3-6

How cool that Jesus repeated His first private miracle for Peter. But this time the disciple didn't drop to his knees and ask for mercy, instead, he called out, "It's the Lord!" then jumped into the water and swam to Him. (Notice he didn't try walking on water here.) Back on the beach, Jesus had a final message for Peter.

> *When they had finished eating, Jesus said to Simon Peter, "Simon son of John, do you love me more than these?" "Yes, Lord," he said, "you know that I love you." Jesus said, "Feed my lambs." Again Jesus said, "Simon son of John, do you love me?" He answered, "Yes, Lord, you know that I love you." Jesus said, "Take care of my sheep." The third time*

he said to him, "Simon son of John, do you love me?" Peter was hurt because Jesus asked him the third time, "Do you love me?" He said, "Lord, you know all things; you know that I love you." Jesus said, "Feed my sheep."

JOHN 21:15-17

Did you notice how many times Jesus asked the question? Yep, three. One for each denial. Jesus not only let Peter know he was forgiven and restored, but also gave him a mission for the rest of his life. This is exactly what Jesus does for anyone who asks for His forgiveness, no matter what sins have been committed. Don't let *your* past hold you back from trying to help people find redemption from *their* past. Jesus forgives you, so let Him! Then go tell others who need to know that their guilt and shame doesn't disqualify them from salvation and forgiveness.

REFLECTION QUESTIONS

What does Jesus' response to Peter teach you about God's forgiveness?

What does Jesus' response to Peter teach you about the feelings of being disqualified or unworthy to tell others what He has done for you?

GOSPELERS ARE DEMON DESTROYERS

The same people who may have seen the worst in us need to hear about the best thing that's ever happened to us.

One of the wildest stories in the Bible is found in Mark 5. If there was ever anyone that we could look at and say, "Well, there's absolutely no way that guy could ever become a gospeler!" it would be this man. But anytime Jesus is involved, you just can't count anyone out.

At the end of Mark 4, we find the story of the storm coming up on a lake while Jesus and the disciples were trying to cross in a boat. While the waves were crashing, what was Jesus doing? Sleeping! Taking a nap—with the disciples freaking out! After they woke Him up, Jesus stood and calmed the storm, amazing them all. But while a physical storm had been stopped, a spiritual storm was about to show up.

On the shore, just as Jesus was climbing out of the boat, a man filled with demons ran up to Him. The local villagers had tried to lock this guy up, but there were so many evil spirits in him that he just snapped the chains and shackles. Mark tells us the man had been living in the cemetery, was naked, cut himself with stones, and howled like an animal at night. Definitely a scary situation. Trying to calm down from the storm, I imagine the disciples' heart rates jumped right back up when they saw this guy running toward them.

Somehow, this man was able to muster up enough strength of will to try and get to Jesus. As he fell to his knees before the Lord, the demons began to beg Jesus to leave them alone. They obviously knew His true identity because they called Him, "Jesus, Son of the Most High God." But as He so often did, Jesus asked a really interesting question: "What is your name?" The demons answered, saying they were called Legion. An interesting fact is a Roman legion of military soldiers was at least four thousand and as many as six thousand in number. If that was the reason for the name, it's no wonder this man was so strong, yet his life was in such horrible shape.

The demons must have known that Jesus wasn't going to allow them to stay in the man, so they started looking for some place to go. Their best option? A herd of two thousand pigs grazing nearby. (Doing the math, that's about three demons per pig.) In commanding them to leave the man, Jesus gave them permission to go into the herd, triggering a crazed stampede. Now, I know for a fact that pigs can be fairly smart animals and are also decent swimmers, but this created a totally different story. When the demons went into the pigs, they bolted, ran down the hillside, and drowned in the same lake where Jesus had just calmed the storm.

But here's where the story goes from shocking and terrifying to mind-blowing and miraculous:

The herdsmen fled to the nearby town and the surrounding countryside, spreading the news as they ran. People rushed out to see what had happened. A crowd soon gathered around Jesus, and they saw the man who had been possessed by the legion of demons. He was sitting there fully clothed and perfectly sane, and they were all afraid.

Mark 5:14-15 NLT

Notice the man's demonic possession is now past tense. Evidently one of the disciples or the locals gave him some clothes to put on. Now, his current state was "perfectly sane." The NIV calls him "dressed and in his right mind." Try and imagine for a moment the incredible relief, joy, and peace this man experienced after Jesus saved and delivered him. While the whole situation scared the crowd, how do you think this rescued man felt?

As Jesus was getting into the boat, the man who had been demon-possessed begged to go with him.

Mark 5:18 NLT

Can you blame him? No! I'd want to stay with Jesus too. But the Lord had a different plan and assignment for him. Jesus had a specific mission for His new disciple.

But Jesus said, "No, go home to your family, and tell them everything the Lord has done for you and how merciful he has been."

Mark 5:19 NLT

The same people who may have seen the worst in us need to hear about the best thing that's ever happened to us. Jesus wanted this man to go back home to the very people who had tried to subdue him with chains and shackles and show them the difference that had been made in his life. Jesus basically told the man to go be a gospeler. Well, how'd he do?

So the man started off to visit the Ten Towns
of that region and began to proclaim
the great things Jesus had done for him;
and everyone was amazed at what he told them.

MARK 5:20 NLT

For anyone who has had a really rough past and struggled to believe they can talk about Jesus, this story should put that concern to rest. Once Jesus has changed any of us, the focus needs to become exactly like this man's—telling everything that the Lord has done and how merciful He has been.

REFLECTION QUESTIONS

Why do you suppose this man might have been able to so quickly overcome his past and start telling everyone what Jesus had done for him?

After reading today's story, do you think it's safe to say that no matter what our past has been, with Jesus, the present and future can have the same outcome as this man's? Explain.

GOSPELERS ARE SHEEP FINDERS

Somewhere, somehow, we shifted from a we-need-to-go mindset to a we-hope-they-come mentality.

Lee Strobel wrote a book called *The Case for Christ* where he details how he set out as a reporter to prove there is no God and wound up becoming a strong believer with a tremendous testimony. Lee is known as a gospeler. I first met him at a conference where he and I were speaking, but I had no idea who he was and had never read his books. When I looked at the options for breakout sessions, I noticed one on evangelism, which obviously interested me. I went straight there without looking at who was teaching.

Truth be told, had I not gone to Lee's session, you would not be reading this book. That hour was the inspiration that started me on a journey of sharing my faith in an even bigger way to a broader audience. The session led me to dedicate myself to help train other Jesus followers in sharing the Gospel. Lee talked about how many churches no longer have dedicated ministries to evangelism or training in how to share our faith.

I thought about how true and telling it is that in our church culture today we pour money, staff, and resources into so many different areas, but rarely have a ministry or plan of action for training church members to go and do the work of evangelism. All those other ministries are no doubt important, but as we've seen, sharing the Good News was Jesus' final command to the church and "of first importance" to the newly-formed church.

There are a lot of different reasons why we don't dedicate time and resources to this all-important ministry. Maybe we miss that Jesus called us all to do the work of evangelism. Maybe we just think the pastors will do it or are paid to do it so they should. Maybe we just hope non-believers will show up on Sunday mornings and hear the Gospel. But, then going back to what I said before, if they come, will they hear the Good News? Somewhere, somehow, we shifted from a we-need-to-go mindset to a we-hope-they-come mentality.

Sitting in Lee Strobel's class that day, I took lots of notes. Months later, when I was able to finally meet him, he told me he thought I wasn't listening because I never looked up. I let him know that was only because I was writing the whole time! Back home, I spoke to the pastors and asked them who was in charge of evangelism at the church. They gave me a strange look, so I made the guess that it must be them! Wouldn't you know it? A month later, I got a call asking if I would be willing to lead a new ministry to teach others how to share their faith. I guess I stepped into that one!

At the time the church asked me, COVID was in full swing, so, of course, I wasn't able to travel at all. I eagerly signed up and got to work, asking around to find out who the "soul winners" were at the church. I had paper and a pen ready to write down their contact info. At a church of several thousand members, you know how many names

I got? Wait for it ... one! Uno. I got one name. *Wow*, I thought, *Well, we can certainly improve on this.*

During the process of leading this ministry, an idea came about to write what would become my book titled *Gospeler*. God was bringing folks together in an effort to take the Gospel to more people. The ministry we started at the church was named 99/ONE and still trains people today to be equipped to share the Gospel to the lost. And it all started with me getting just one name.

In Matthew 18, Jesus gave us a short parable about the "99/ONE" and how important the "one" is to God.

> *What do you think? If a man owns a hundred sheep, and one of them wanders away, will he not leave the ninety-nine on the hills and go to look for the one that wandered off? And if he finds it, truly I tell you, he is happier about that one sheep than about the ninety-nine that did not wander off. In the same way your Father in heaven is not willing that any of these little ones should perish.*
>
> MATTHEW 18:12-14

I believe those of us in the church sometimes forget about the one. When you look at where we spend our efforts and money, it all tends to go toward the "99" side. That's why I know that *Gospeler* and this *Gospel Courage* devotional are not for the mass-market or the big events. I'm in no way against those, because I speak at plenty of them. But this is for "the one"—the *one* who's reading and trying to get better at always being prepared for the *one* lost person; the person we all were at *one* time before we were with the "99" other sheep.

Luke ends his account of the Parable of the Lost Sheep with these words from Jesus:

> *In the same way, I tell you, there is rejoicing in the presence of the angels of God over one sinner who repents.*
>
> LUKE 15:10

My hope is that more churches will be willing to start new ministries focused on the Gospel, to step up and make the changes necessary to prioritize seeking and saving the lost in an intentional way. Lee Strobel was one new believer who was able to completely ditch a mindset he had his whole life, then let that reborn life turn into a global ministry where changing minds and hearts for Christ is the number one objective. I was challenged through his teaching to increase my focus and efforts to include evangelism even more than I had. So, you are next! Like Jesus, you can go "leave the ninety-nine on the hills and go to look for the one who wandered off." Always be ready to do whatever it takes to go after that one.

REFLECTION QUESTIONS

Does your church or circle of Christian friends place much focus on sharing with non-believers? If your answer is little to none, what steps can you take to change that?

In what ways does Jesus' story of the sheep in Matthew 18 inspire you to be a gospeler?

GOSPELERS ARE SEED SPREADERS

Have you ever thought about what you're investing in this life to prepare for life after this?

Jesus was the world's greatest teacher. He could take simple concepts and teach them to people so they could understand. Imagine experiencing eternity, coming to earth, and then trying to explain all this in human terms. Rather than blow everyone's minds, He often used simple, everyday stories to help us understand the Kingdom of God. That's a good approach for us as well. Don't try and make all this so complicated. In Matthew 13, Jesus gives us a parable that is all about the gospeler's mission of getting the Good News out, where He talks about farmers, seeds, soil, birds, roots, and ultimately, multiplication.

Listen! A farmer went out to plant some seeds.
As he scattered them across his field,
some seeds fell on a footpath, and the birds
came and ate them. Other seeds fell on shallow
soil with underlying rock. The seeds sprouted
quickly because the soil was shallow.
But the plants soon wilted under the hot sun,
and since they didn't have deep roots, they died.
Other seeds fell among thorns that grew up and
choked out the tender plants. Still other seeds fell on
fertile soil, and they produced a crop that was thirty,

sixty, and even a hundred times
as much as had been planted!

MATTHEW 13:3-8 NLT

The seed sower did two things: First, went out into the field where the seed was needed. Second, "scattered them across the field," throwing seed anywhere and everywhere. Bottom line—the sower's job is just to throw seed, not be responsible for the outcome. The sower can't control the soil, just the seed.

As gospelers, we don't pick and choose or discriminate about who gets the Gospel or where it goes. We just throw seed by having conversations about Him. Yes, there are going to be those times when the message will fall on deaf ears and get rejected. But you can't know until you try. There's no reaping until you sow. There's no harvest without planting seeds. There were very few times that Jesus actually explained one of His parables, but for this one, He did.

Now listen to the explanation of the parable about the farmer planting seeds: The seed that fell on the footpath represents those who hear the message about the Kingdom and don't understand it. Then the evil one comes and snatches away the seed that was planted in their hearts. The seed on the rocky soil represents those who hear the message and immediately receive it with joy. But since they don't have deep roots, they don't last long. They fall away as soon as they have problems or are persecuted for believing God's word. The seed that fell among the thorns represents those who hear God's word, but all too quickly the message is crowded out by the worries of this life and the lure of wealth, so no fruit is produced. The seed that fell on good soil represents those who truly hear and understand God's word and produce a harvest of thirty, sixty, or even a hundred times as much as had been planted!

MATTHEW 13:18-23 NLT

So, what could the sower have done differently? Nothing. Only God and the person who heard the Gospel had anything to do with the result, proving we are never the one who saves. We are simply the messengers, the gospelers. But there will be those times when we need to go back and throw seed in the same place again. One example for me was when I found out that a good friend, Bill, was diagnosed with cancer. I had tried to share Jesus with him many times, but whenever I would bring up anything spiritual, he would just say, "Let he who hath not sinned cast the first stone," from the story in John 8. In other words, "Willie, I don't want to hear what you have to say about God." But after his diagnosis, I felt an urgency and had to keep sowing for Bill's sake.

On a business trip in New York, we were going over a deal in the back of an Uber. I decided it was time once again to get the Gospel to Bill. But this time I tried something new. I told him I thought he only had a few years left to live. I made the prediction of when his life on this earth could come to an end based on his age, habits, and general statistics. What I said definitely seemed to get Bill's attention. Then I asked, "Have you ever thought about what you're investing in this life to prepare for life *after* this?" This time, I could see I hit a nerve. As we pulled up to the hotel, he asked if I could keep talking. Grabbing my Bible, I went to his suite.

Bill told me he had come to faith in college, but, over the years, that all seemed to vanish, just like one of the seeds that never took root. But Jesus never said we couldn't throw more seeds into the same soil. So, that's what I did. As we were reading in the New Testament, he stood to his feet and announced, "I'm getting baptized!" I said, "Well, Bill, it's midnight in New York City, but I'll go see if I can find some water." He replied, "No, not tonight. I have to tell everyone I know."

Back home, Bill called with a date and told me he wanted to be baptized in a lake on his property. When I got there, I realized he had done exactly what he said he would do. People were there from LA to New York. He gathered everyone up and announced, "Willie, tell them what you told me in that hotel room in New York City!" So, I shared the story of Jesus with the crowd. After I baptized Bill, he shouted at the group standing on the bank, "Whoever's next, come on in!" To my surprise, people started streaming into that lake fully clothed, one after another. By the time we were done, twenty-four people responded to the Gospel!

Based on the parable of the sower, only about one in four times of sharing the Gospel will bring a harvest. My own experience over the years bears that out as well. That means we need to understand only about twenty-five percent of the people we talk with will respond with a yes. But, like Bill's story, when the seed falls on fertile soil, it can produce "a harvest of thirty, sixty, or even a hundred times as much as had been planted." A lake full of people!

REFLECTION QUESTIONS

What does Jesus' story about the sower tell you about your role in the spread of the Gospel?

What does Jesus' explanation of what happened to the seed tell you about His role?

GOSPELERS ARE NOT DWELLERS

Because life is short, that is why our mission is so valuable.

I have noticed in life that discouragement is a critical component in shutting us down. Many things can be discouraging, especially people! Here's the deal—you can learn, get prepared, and committed to share your faith, but when, not if, you face discouragement, it can neutralize your entire mission. Even the numbers we looked at yesterday with the sower and the soil at only twenty-five percent giving a yes can seem pretty discouraging. For context, what if you worked a full-time week, but only got twenty-five percent of your paycheck? How long would you last?

An important thing to realize is that when you believe in Jesus, you have to also believe there are evil forces at work that don't want anyone following Jesus and changing their lives. One of their favorite tools to use is discouragement. No one faced this more than Jesus Christ Himself. All He did was good, while negativity constantly followed Him—from downright evil folks to supposedly "godly" people. I cannot imagine how discouraging it would be to experience rejection and hostility from the very people He came to give His life for. Yet, Jesus never seemed to dwell on those things, but just kept moving forward on His mission.

A great example is in Luke 5 after Jesus had invited a despised tax collector named Matthew, also known as Levi, to follow Him. Matthew threw a big dinner party inviting all his old friends to meet Jesus. That's a great gospeler move, by the way, to plan a big eating gig and use it to try and get the Good News to people.

After this, Jesus went out and saw a tax collector by the name of Levi sitting at his tax booth. "Follow me," Jesus said to him, and Levi got up, left everything and followed him. Then Levi held a great banquet for Jesus at his house, and a large crowd of tax collectors and others were eating with them.

LUKE 5:27-29

But the Pharisees, a group of religious hypocrites, somehow saw the guest list and confronted Jesus about His choice of who to hang out with. Now, why would they even care? You should also be ready to run into this when you start sharing your faith.

But the Pharisees and the teachers of the law who belonged to their sect complained to his disciples, "Why do you eat and drink with tax collectors and sinners?" Jesus answered them, "It is not the healthy who need a doctor, but the sick. I have not come to call the righteous, but sinners to repentance."

LUKE 5:30-32

Jesus squashes the negativity by doubling-down on His mission. He knows by the way these guys conduct themselves that God's message will never get through them to the people who need it. In fact, the Pharisees may be the very reason others may never come to God because they would never want to be like them. Again, Jesus doesn't dwell on their criticism or second-guess Himself, He just moves on. Jesus knows His mission is reaching sinners, which can be discouraging enough as it is. To test His analogy, go hang out at a doctor's office or emergency room and see how difficult it is to not be discouraged.

James 1:2 says, "Consider it pure joy, my brothers and sisters, whenever you face trials of many kinds." James tells us to reverse the negative to a positive, to not just joy, but pure joy. The kind of joy the Holy Spirit helps us grow as fruit. We know the opposite of discourage is courage. But you can't see courage in anyone until there is action. You don't just look at someone and say, "He looks courageous." No, it's inside us, just like the Holy Spirit. When courage and the Holy Spirit team up in our hearts, we become dynamic ambassadors for Christ, moving past the roadblocks that evil puts in place to try and discourage us. Have no doubt that we are in a battle that can only be won with Gospel courage. Battlefields are not made for dwelling. No one wants to stay there. They are made for movement, to engage the enemy and press on in the mission.

We are dwellers of this earth, only here for a short time, then moving on. Because life is short, that is why our mission is so valuable. The gospeler's message is the very hope of Heaven with the Gospel fueling our courage. The people who still need to hear the Good News dwell on the things of this earth and will be left with an emptiness and dissatisfaction. The writer of Hebrews puts it this way:

> *For this world is not our home; we are looking forward to our everlasting home in heaven. With Jesus' help we will continually offer our sacrifice of praise to God by telling others of the glory of his name.*
>
> Hebrews 13:14-15 TLB

One of the best ways to show praise to our God is by telling others about Him and His everlasting home He's prepared that is waiting on us. Just like the men and women in the time of Jesus, let the resistance to the Gospel fuel your courage. Don't hate the ones who discourage you, just share the Good News with them and pray they too can believe in the hope of eternity. Be positive, be courageous, and be on mission with the Holy Spirit leading the way.

REFLECTION QUESTIONS

Has discouragement affected your own faith? If so, how much of that was from other people, Christians or not? Explain.

Have you had moments you've gotten discouraged trying to share your faith? How did you respond?

YOU DON'T NEED A BATH

Any baptism that occurs without Jesus is just a temporary event. With Jesus, it's an eternal experience.

Today, I want to offer one final look at baptism to help us cover the potential concerns and questions folks can have on this important step of obedience to Jesus. But there are also times that conversations on this topic may help someone realize they don't fully understand the Gospel. When I read Scripture, I always ask, "Why is this in the Bible? There must be a reason." When I looked at the possible answer to that question for the story in Acts 19:1-7, I discovered how it can help some people find clarity.

While Apollos was at Corinth, Paul took the road through the interior and arrived at Ephesus. There he found some disciples and asked them, "Did you receive the Holy Spirit when you believed?"

ACTS 19:1-2

First, notice what Paul called the people he encountered in Ephesus: *disciples*. These were not lost people or religious leaders opposing the Gospel, but folks who clearly identified with Paul. But, even with Scripture describing them that way, what was the first thing Paul did when he met them? He started the conversation by asking a question. While we aren't told why, he asked: "Did you receive the Holy Spirit when you believed?"

Maybe something they had done or said, or something Paul had heard about them, made him think they did not have the Spirit. But, as usual, he was dead-on, because their response was quick and clear:

> *They answered, "No, we have not even heard that there is a Holy Spirit."*
>
> ACTS 19:2

Look where Paul goes next as he continued his questions but got more specific.

> *So Paul asked, "Then what baptism did you receive?" "John's baptism," they replied. Paul said, "John's baptism was a baptism of repentance. He told the people to believe in the one coming after him, that is, in Jesus."*
>
> ACTS 19:3-4

After understanding that they had responded to and received John the Baptist's message of repentance of sin, Paul made it clear that there was a bigger picture and more to the story. The One John preached and prophesied about—Jesus—had come. While these believers in Ephesus were serious about repenting of their sins, without Jesus, there was no salvation. So, what was their response to Paul's connection and clarification?

On hearing this, they were baptized in the name of the Lord Jesus.

ACTS 19:5

Once they understood the truth and the connection between Jesus and the forgiveness of their sin, they were baptized again. This time, "in the name of the Lord Jesus." This passage can be helpful to folks who may have a similar story with a previous baptism or who haven't yet fully understood all the Gospel means. Paul made sure they knew about Jesus and then took the next and final step of baptizing them again. As with any baptism that occurs without Jesus, it's just a temporary event. With Jesus, it's an eternal experience. When I read this story, the question I ask is, "Why did he feel the need to baptize them again? Why not just tell them so they understand the difference?" Like I said earlier, there has to be a reason, and it must have mattered.

Later, in 1 Peter 3, once again, we see Jesus' death and resurrection connected to baptism. We also see the Old Testament connected to the New Testament with a new term describing baptism:

For it is better, if it is God's will, to suffer for doing good than for doing evil. For Christ also suffered once for sins, the righteous for the unrighteous, to bring you to God. He was put to death in the body but made alive in the Spirit. After being made alive, he went and made proclamation to the imprisoned spirits—to those who were disobedient long ago when God waited patiently in the days of Noah while the ark was being built. In it only a few people, eight in all, were saved through water, and this water symbolizes baptism that now saves you also—not the removal of dirt from the body but the pledge of a clear conscience toward God. It saves you by the resurrection of Jesus Christ, who has gone into heaven and is at God's right hand—with angels, authorities and powers in submission to him.

1 PETER 3:17-22

He says, "not the removal of dirt from the body." In other words: You don't need a bath! Baptism is an inner, spiritual washing. Peter described baptism as "the pledge of a clear conscience towards God." Like we talked about in Day 30, I have had Gospel conversations with a lot of people who struggle with guilt and shame for things they have done. More than anything, they want a clear conscience to be able to live at peace with themselves. They have struggled their way through life wanting to be right with God, but not knowing how. Honestly, there are a lot of folks sitting in pews every Sunday morning who are still searching for that clear conscience and personal peace, yet still can't seem to understand the answer.

Just like Paul helped the people in Ephesus realize that they didn't have the Holy Spirit, we can help people walk through their questions; to find the real problem and also the only real answer; to believe what Peter said, that we are saved "by the resurrection of Jesus Christ, who has gone into heaven and is at God's right hand." Besides the people who have never heard the Gospel, we have to be ready to help those who only have *some* of the truth, but don't yet know *all* of the truth. They need the Helper that God sent to empower them to live like Jesus.

REFLECTION QUESTIONS

What is one way that today's passage helped you understand how even those who say they believe may not fully understand the Gospel?

____

____

____

____

____

From all the passages and stories we have shared about baptism, what is one truth you have learned?

____

____

____

____

____

BE READY TO REASON

We have too many Christians who can tell someone what they believe, but they can't tell anyone why they believe it.

One thing I've learned in sharing the Gospel with others is that not everyone comes to the conversation from the same starting place. People come with all sorts of life experiences, questions, and objections. Some people I share with have a level of belief in who Jesus is and some don't. Some have past church experiences, good and bad, and some don't have any. Some are familiar with the Bible, and some aren't. And some don't want to hear about it at all.

Because of all these variables, we need to be prepared to share the Good News of Jesus with anyone God puts in our path. That's part of the process of maturing as a gospeler. Regardless of whatever life experiences others bring and whatever objections we face, we have Good News the world needs to hear. That's why I love the verse I shared earlier:

Always be prepared to give an answer to everyone who asks you to give the reason for the hope that you have.

1 PETER 3:15

There are too many Christians who can tell someone what they believe, but they can't tell anyone why they believe it. They are terrified to share their faith with others, especially strangers, because of the questions or objections they might face, wondering, "What if they ask me something I can't answer? What if they don't believe in God or the Bible? What do I say then?"

The good news is, we're not expected to have all the answers. God does the work of drawing people to salvation, not us. But, as we grow in sharing the Gospel, we need to be able to reason with folks who don't believe. Trusting Jesus doesn't mean we have to have blind faith. We can learn to present solid reasons of why we believe what we believe.

Today, I want to take a look at how Paul shared the Gospel in a city called Thessalonica:

> *When Paul and his companions had passed through Amphipolis and Apollonia, they came to Thessalonica, where there was a Jewish synagogue. As was his custom, Paul went into the synagogue, and on three Sabbath days he reasoned with them from the Scriptures, explaining and proving that the Messiah had to suffer and rise from the dead. "This Jesus I am proclaiming to you is the Messiah," he said. Some of the Jews were persuaded and joined Paul and Silas, as did a large number of God-fearing Greeks and quite a few prominent women.*
>
> Acts 17:1-4

Notice what Paul did. These were Jewish people, so he used the Scriptures to reason with them at the synagogue. He showed how all of the stories and prophesies in the Old Testament were fulfilled in Jesus. We discussed that back on Day 29, but I want you to notice here that Paul was starting where the people were at. Because they studied and followed the Torah, Paul used that to provide them with many evidences that Jesus was who He claimed to be.

Even for someone who doesn't believe in the Bible, Jesus' fulfillment of prophesies that were written centuries before Him is a powerful testament of who He is. There are over 300 prophecies in the Old Testament that point to Jesus, telling us the family line He would come through, the city He would be born in, the virgin birth, details of His ministry, His miracles, His death, and even pointing to how He would die. Isaiah prophesied in Isaiah 53:5 that He would be "pierced for our transgression." Psalm 22 refers to His hands and feet being pierced, and people casting lots for His clothes (Psalm 22:16-18). This was hundreds of years before crucifixion even existed!

Let's shift to see how Paul shared the Gospel with some very different people—Greek philosophers in the city of Athens—some of the most highly educated guys on the planet who loved to debate.

Paul then stood up in the meeting of the Areopagus and said: "People of Athens! I see that in every way you are very religious. For as I walked around and looked carefully at your objects of worship, I even found an altar with this inscription: to an unknown god. So you are ignorant of the very thing you worship—and this is what I am going to proclaim to you."

ACTS 17:22-23

Man, I love that! Again, Paul started right where they were and began to testify about the God of the universe. They didn't believe in Scripture, so he didn't begin there. He used one of the objects of their worship, a stone altar to an unknown god, and then pointed them to the one true God. The result was that some mocked him, but some became believers.

The same is true for us when we share. Not only did over 300 prophesies get it right, but creation itself declares God. Paul writes in his first chapter to the church in Rome:

For since the creation of the world God's invisible qualities—his eternal power and divine nature—have been clearly seen, being understood from what has been made, so that people are without excuse.

ROMANS 1:20

When we share with others, we can follow Paul's example by understanding where they're at and using the evidence around us. Our very world points to God and testifies of an intelligent design and a personal Creator. People you talk with can generally agree on two realities—our world has a lot of beauty, but there is also a lot of darkness. There are things that inspire us, lift us up, and move our souls, but there is also brokenness and evil that seem to make no sense. Some people I share with bring up evil as evidence against God. But, for me, these things just point to the fact that there is a spiritual battle beyond what we can see. Evil reminds us exactly what the Bible tells us: there is sin in this world, which should cause us to long for Heaven and bring as many folks with us as we can.

The more we study and observe around us, the better chance we have of breaking through someone's objections and reaching them with the Gospel. So, would you be prepared to share with someone who doesn't believe that God exists? Or Jesus never walked the earth? Or He really wasn't raised from the dead? If not, then it's time to do what Peter said and take time to prepare to give a reason for your hope. Today, we have so many great resources available to help us deepen in our faith. Because we never know who God will send to us, we must be ready with any help for the person who might turn to Jesus.

REFLECTION QUESTIONS

Have you ever had someone ask you questions about your faith that you didn't feel prepared to answer? How did you respond?

What does Paul's method of reasoning tell you about the importance of knowing Scripture and looking to God's available answers like creation to point people to Jesus?

SHAPING AND SHAKING

What if God is trying to shake you up a bit to shake off what is not eternal in you?

Have you ever felt like God was shaking things up in your life? Have you ever felt like He was shaping you for some higher purpose? While I have experienced both, I'll be honest, shaking usually involves more pain than shaping. Sometimes these seasons are hard at first, but soon end up being good. Other times, we find ourselves in some unexpected and unpredictable valley and our only choice is to just keep walking forward in faith.

In Day 5 and Day 24, we looked at Acts 16 where Paul and Silas were praying and singing in a prison cell at midnight. God decided to shake things up, literally. A "violent earthquake" shook the very foundation of the prison. So much so that the cell doors flew open, and everyone's chains came loose. A terrifying event at first that ended up becoming a blessing for Paul, Silas, the jailer and his family. But a *shaking* had to happen before the *shaping* could begin.

In Exodus 19, as Moses and the Israelites stood before God at the foot of the mountain, verse 18 says, "the whole mountain trembled violently." In 1 Kings 19, when the prophet Elijah was on Mount Horeb in the presence of God, there was a powerful wind, fire, and an earthquake. In Matthew 27, when Christ gave up His spirit, the earth shook. Verse 54 tells us the centurions guarding Jesus were terrified by an earthquake. Bottom line—there is plenty of evidence in the Bible that God will shake things up to accomplish His purposes.

So often, for God to get us into the place to shape us by His Spirit, first He has to shake us. He has to get us out of our comfort zones and status quo patterns to take us where He can work in and through us. Then He can shape or transform us more into the image of Jesus. Even if we may be the only ones to feel the shaking, we know it is very real.

There are a number of places in Scripture where pottery is used as a metaphor for our lives. Isaiah 64:8 says, "Yet you, Lord, are our Father. We are the clay, you are the potter; we are all the work of your hand." So, if we truly are just human clay, why does God need to shake up our lives? Shaping, okay, but shaking? Why? The author of Hebrews offers us a better understanding.

See to it that you do not refuse him who speaks. If they did not escape when they refused him who warned them on earth, how much less will we, if we turn away from him who warns us from heaven? At that time his voice shook the earth, but now he has promised, "Once more I will shake not only the earth but also the heavens." The words "once more" indicate the removing of what can be shaken—that is, created things—so that what cannot be shaken may remain. Therefore, since we are receiving a kingdom that cannot be shaken, let us be thankful, and so worship God acceptably with reverence and awe, for our "God is a consuming fire."

HEBREWS 12:25-29

Only what "cannot be shaken" will remain. Only in the refining fire of God can we as clay become purified and strengthened, a necessary process to be ready for His work here and for Heaven when our mission is accomplished.

Maybe you feel like you really want to share the Good News with people, but you're in a place right now where you don't want to be? A place you feel like you didn't choose? Or maybe you did choose it and that's why you are in a battle? Maybe your life has been, or is currently being, shaken? If that is the case, I totally get that it is easy to put a negative spin on whatever is happening to you right now. But, here's a question to help you look at your circumstances from a different perspective through a different lens.

What if God is trying to *shake you* up a bit to *shake off* what is not eternal in you? What if His ultimate goal is to get you on mission to get out the Gospel? To bless you through relationships and conversations with others that you never imagined you might have? To be a part of helping people find real, authentic, and eternal answers? Perhaps you have just been going through the motions for many years and need a revision of your mission, a reset of your purpose.

Through the mountains and the valleys, through the dark days and the glorious days, we have to keep in mind that God doesn't just free us from our sin for our sake. He doesn't change our lives just so we can go back to our old ways and take the easy road. He has a purpose for every one of us. From the day we say yes to Jesus to the day we enter Heaven, we are on mission with Him. We live life for Him and His glory. We live life for others to come to know Him.

REFLECTION QUESTIONS

Has there been a time in your life where God has shaken you? Explain.

Is there any area of your life where you feel like God is shaping you right now? If so, what do you think He may be preparing you for? Explain.

NEVER GIVE UP

Our job isn't to save, but to share.

I really wish I could say that every person I have ever shared the Gospel with had said yes right away. I would love to be able to tell you, with every single one of them, that we prayed and then I took them out to the water to get baptized. But that wouldn't be true. One thing *is* for sure, with every Gospel conversation I have, that is my hope and prayer.

I've had plenty of folks tell me their stories, read the Scriptures with me, and appear to understand what Jesus has done for them, but then say no. Some never actually said no, but, for some reason, they just weren't ready at that moment. When Pastor Bill went to Dad's bar to share the Gospel, after he was finished telling him about Jesus, Dad looked at him and said, "I'll keep that in mind, preacher." So, Pastor Bill left Arkansas to drive home to West Monroe empty-handed, so to speak. He may have thought my dad let the Gospel go in one ear and out the other. I've often wondered about Bill's conversation with God as he was driving home. Did he say, "Well, Lord, I'm not sure what that was all about, but I did what Phil's sister, Jan, asked me to do. I told her brother about You and how You can save Him"?

When we decide to be gospelers, when we hear either "no" or "not now," we can't get upset with the person or feel like we wasted our time. And we certainly can't get frustrated with the Lord. We have to exercise the same faith that drove us to share, the same faith we told the person about, and then trust God with the outcome. That's when we need to keep in mind the truth we find in Isaiah:

> *As the rain and the snow come down*
> *from heaven, and do not return to it without*
> *watering the earth and making it bud and flourish,*
> *so that it yields seed for the sower and bread*
> *for the eater, so is my word that goes out from*
> *my mouth: It will not return to me empty,*
> *but will accomplish what I desire and*
> *achieve the purpose for which I sent it.*
>
> Isaiah 55:10-11

Sometimes we water, sometimes we plant seeds, and sometimes we get to harvest. I've had some people reach back out to me after they had time to think and process everything we talked about, sometimes even months or years later. They told me they were ready to believe Jesus, accept the Gospel, and be baptized. That's exactly what happened with Dad. He stayed true to his word with Pastor Bill. He "kept it in mind." Less than a year later, he drove back home and said he was ready to give his life to Jesus. Dad obviously had a little farther to go to hit bottom, but once he did, because of Pastor Bill's faithfulness, he knew where to go and what to do. And, by that time, Mom had received the Gospel, and they started their new life together with Jesus.

We have to constantly remind ourselves that God doesn't save people on our timetable, but on His. Our job isn't to save, but to share. Afterwards, we pray; we don't push. Because, to repeat, we're just the messengers and the message is His. One of the amazing things about the Good News is that it not only can change and transform a person's life, but potentially their entire family. I am one of those. And then there are times when that family will forever change the legacy of future generations. That's certainly what happened to us Robertsons.

That is the very reason why I never give up on people who may say no to Jesus at first. I don't write the person off, but I hang in there with them. I always remember my dad's story. Another huge motivation for me is thinking about how many people that person could ultimately end up leading to Jesus when they do say *yes*.

In the Gospel of Luke, chapter 18 we find the story of "the rich, young ruler." One day, this man walked up to Jesus and asked how he could inherit eternal life. When Jesus referred to the Ten Commandments, He listed number six through number nine, then jumped up to number five, and closed with "Love your neighbor as yourself." Because Jesus was always so specific in His dealings with anyone, we have to trust there was some reason behind His choice of which commandments He brought up. Here's the rest of that encounter:

"All these I have kept since I was a boy,"
he said. When Jesus heard this, he said to him,
"You still lack one thing. Sell everything you have

and give to the poor, and you will have treasure in heaven. Then come, follow me."

Luke 18:21-22

Jesus was very intentional in what He said to him. He knew how it would be difficult for this man to follow Him. This is the "gathering the story" part from Jesus. When you talk to people, you might also hear those areas that are going to be tough for them to let go of for transformation to take place. It's amazing that this man actually got a personal invitation from Jesus to follow Him. Peter got this same offer, and we have already covered how he turned out. But what happened in this story?

When he heard this, he became very sad, because he was very wealthy.

Luke 18:23

Even Jesus got *no* for an answer. He did not keep bringing it up over and over. He didn't second-guess or lower the bar because He knew how valuable it would be for a rich young ruler to join the group. He only wants people who are all-in. That's why we just move on and keep throwing out seeds. Jesus threw out a seed that day. But who knows? Maybe the guy came back around later. Maybe he was one of the three thousand who heard Peter preach. Maybe like my dad, he "kept it in mind" and eventually believed in Jesus.

REFLECTION QUESTIONS

Who is someone that you never thought would come to faith but finally surrendered to Jesus? What do you think was the turning point?

Do you need to be set free by accepting the truth that you can't save someone, no matter how hard you try? Is there someone you've been praying for or sharing with, and you feel the burden of their salvation? Write out your thoughts.

YOUR JESUS FAMILY TREE

If you can celebrate the fact that you follow Jesus today, that means someone in your life was a gospeler.

The most important thing that has been and will ever be passed down in the Robertson family was what millions of people saw every week at the end of each *Duck Dynasty* episode. No matter what crazy thing had just been shown for the past half hour, when we gathered around Dad and Mom's table, our faith in Jesus was the focus. That is the one thing that affects every single part of my life. The one thing that has helped me in my career, my marriage, raising my children, with my friends, my travels, and pretty much everything I am connected to in life. That one thing gives me joy when life gets tough; encourages me when I fail; and offers me meaning and purpose. And best of all, gives me hope for the future and for eternity. That one thing is the Gospel of Jesus Christ.

Today, I want you to not think about your *family* genealogy, but your *Gospel* genealogy. Back in Day 26, I gave you the opportunity to write out your story in how you came to follow Jesus. As you completed the sentence: "I came to know Jesus by/through," there's a high probability you mentioned a person or persons. Even if it has been many years since the day you first believed, you can likely recall the name and how he or she helped you. If you can celebrate the fact that you follow Jesus today, that means someone in your life was a gospeler. Someone was willing to have a Gospel conversation with you. Even if you watched a preacher on TV or online to hear the Good News, likely someone at some point sat down to help you understand your commitment and answer your questions. The vast majority of us who have received the Gospel had a person in our lives who obeyed the Lord and loved us enough to share that God loves us and wants to save us.

Here's the cool legacy part of your story, your Gospel genealogy. Whoever shared with you had someone share with them. And the person before them. And the person before them. Have you ever thought about all of the people that God used to get His message of redemption to you? It's your Jesus family tree. Faithful men and women passed on the Good News, over and over again, for two centuries until the message reached you! This incredible movement we call the church—the body of Christ—goes all the way back to the days of the New Testament. For two thousand years, men and women all across the globe have been faithful to fulfill Jesus' Great Commission.

Over all those generations, the spread of the Gospel has been dependent on one thing—people who love Jesus enough to tell others about Him. Back in Day 19, our Bible passage was Romans 10:9-10. Today, I want to drop down a few verses and talk about what Paul said next:

For "Everyone who calls on the name of the Lord will be saved." But how can they call on him to save them unless they believe in him? And how can they believe in him if they have never heard about him? And how can they hear about him unless someone tells them?

Romans 10:13-14 NLT

So, who are "they" in the beginning of each of the three questions? The answer is anyone who needs to call on the name of the Lord to be saved. Those who have not heard must be told so they can hear before they can believe and be saved. Paul said people need a gospeler. One of the reasons I love verse 14 is because he speaks to the heart of the Gospel and what God has called all believers to do. We have been given the incredible privilege and responsibility to partner with Him to reach people with the Good News of Jesus Christ. Back in Day 4, we read Luke 19:10, "For the Son of Man came to seek and save the lost." Paul's questions in verse 14 connect right back to Christ's mission and the commission He has given us.

When Paul asks, "How are those who need to be saved going to call on Him?" and "How can they believe in Him?" and "How can they hear the message?" the answer is obvious. They can't and they won't unless we go and tell them. Now, I'm not sure if I've ever thought of anyone's feet being beautiful, but look at what verse 15 tells us:

How beautiful are the feet of messengers who bring good news!

Romans 10:15 NLT

Notice why the feet are beautiful. Because the message was taken to those who need to call on the name of the Lord to be saved. The messenger had to be proactive to go and tell. By now, through the pages of this devotional, I believe you have been given enough information and inspiration that you can go and be part of someone else's Gospel story, become a part of someone's Gospel genealogy.

God has given you His Holy Spirit to guide you and also offer you the boldness you need to share about the most important thing in your life—your Lord and your salvation. My hope and prayer is that you begin to step out in faith to discover how amazing it is to know that someday, someone (or many people) may be able to write down your name when they share their story.

REFLECTION QUESTIONS

Who was your gospeler and what were the circumstances around how that person shared the Gospel with you?

How does considering your Gospel genealogy both in the past and beyond you, to continue your Jesus family tree, encourage you to share the Good News?

THE LAST THING

We have more opportunities now than ever before to share the Gospel.

As we close out these forty days, I want to say thank you for taking this journey with me. I hope that it's challenged you to be a gospeler and also given you greater courage to know that you have everything you need to share the Good News of Jesus with other people. Take courage because you have the Holy Spirit, God's Word, and your own testimony. On this last day, I want to look again at one of my favorite gospelers in all the Bible—Stephen. Remember, Stephen was one of the seven chosen in Acts 6, and, immediately, we see that he was on fire for Jesus. The first verse mentioning him by himself says: "Now Stephen, a man full of God's grace and power, performed great wonders and signs among the people" (Acts 6:8).

Stephen was soon arrested for being a gospeler. The religious folks were dead-set on doing whatever it took to make him stop sharing about Jesus. He was brought before the high priest and the religious leaders. Instead of cowering down before these powerful people, Stephen was full of the Holy Spirit and began to speak with boldness—with true Gospel courage. The result is the longest sermon we have recorded in the book of Acts.

Stephen used his opportunity to show them, through Scripture, starting all the way back with Abraham, that they were rejecting the work of God, just as they had for centuries. He reminded them that the leaders of the past they look up to, like Moses, predicted the coming of the Messiah and were rejected in the same way Jesus was rejected. But God was always faithful and continued to carry out His plan all the way to the coming of Jesus. Stephen's strongest criticisms came at the end of his speech:

You stiff-necked people! Your hearts and ears are still uncircumcised. You are just like your ancestors: You always resist the Holy Spirit! Was there ever a prophet your ancestors did not persecute? They even killed those who predicted the coming of the Righteous One. And now you have betrayed and murdered him—you who have received the law that was given through angels but have not obeyed it.

ACTS 7:51-53

Stephen declared the truth regardless of the audience and despite the cost. He didn't speak his opinion, but he used Scripture to prove that God was always moving, and that Jesus was the Son of God who had come to lay down His life. What was their response?

When the members of the Sanhedrin heard this, they were furious and gnashed their teeth at him. But Stephen, full of the Holy Spirit, looked up to heaven and saw the glory of God, and Jesus standing at the right hand of God. "Look," he said, "I see heaven open and the Son of Man standing at the right hand of God." At this they covered their ears and, yelling at the top of their voices, they all rushed at him, dragged him out of the city and began to stone him. Meanwhile, the witnesses laid their coats at the feet of a young man named Saul. While they were stoning him, Stephen prayed, "Lord Jesus, receive my spirit." Then he fell on his knees and cried out, "Lord, do not hold this sin against them." When he had said this, he fell asleep.

ACTS 7:54-60

What Stephen spoke to those religious leaders was the Gospel—Jesus was "the Righteous One" who had been prophesied, was betrayed and killed by them, and was now glorified and standing at the right hand of God. Stephen became the first Christian martyr as he laid down his life for his Lord. We have such a long line of gospelers who have continued to proclaim the Good News generation after generation at all costs.

Hopefully, you'll never face that kind of persecution, but I can promise you that if you live your life as a gospeler, you're sure to face some roadblocks. Maybe yours will look like mocking, ridicule, rejection, being called close-minded, or a religious bigot. Maybe the obstacles will be your own fear or your desire for comfort and just keeping life status quo.

I believe we have more opportunities now than ever before to share the Gospel. We can jump in a car or on a plane and get just about anywhere on the globe. Endless platforms exist to communicate. It's easy to complain about the negativity online or on social media, but I think that's where we need to just bring a little light. You may not be the one preaching to a crowd of religious elites or going to the most remote parts of the world, but you have a voice, you have places and ways you can get the Good News out. Start with where God has placed you, what God has given you, and who God has given you. Be courageous and begin where you are.

There are a lot of great things in life you can be known for. My prayer for you is that more than anything else, you'll be known as a gospeler.

REFLECTION QUESTIONS

For our final reflection questions, I want to encourage you to make some practical commitments to be better prepared to share the Good News.

Do you need to commit to more Bible study to be better prepared to share?

Are there people you need to share with (family, friends, neighbors, coworkers)?

Are there places you need to begin to share (work, school, gym, church outreach events)?

Do you need to be bolder to share your faith on platforms such as social media?

Using the questions above as prompts, write out three to four commitments you can make to be a gospeler as you go forward:

SCRIPTURE PASSAGES FOR SHARING THE GOSPEL

THE "LINE OF FAITH" FROM DAY 12

Love Joy Peace Gentleness Self-Control

GALATIANS 5:19-24

Immorality Impurity Hatred Selfish Ambition

ACTS OF SINFUL NATURE: GALATIANS 5:19-21

The acts of the flesh are obvious: sexual immorality, impurity and debauchery; idolatry and witchcraft; hatred, discord, jealousy, fits of rage, selfish ambition, dissensions, factions and envy; drunkenness, orgies, and the like. I warn you, as I did before, that those who live like this will not inherit the kingdom of God.

FRUIT OF THE SPIRIT: GALATIANS 5:22-23

But the fruit of the Spirit is love, joy, peace, forbearance, kindness, goodness, faithfulness, gentleness and self-control. Against such things there is no law.

"MY STORY AND THE GOSPEL" FROM DAY 25

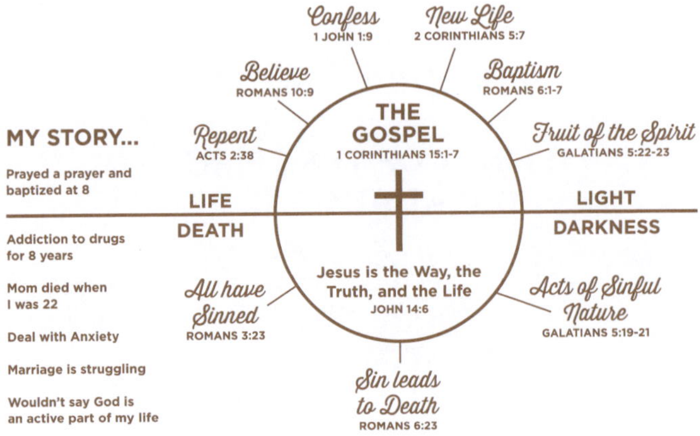

THE GOSPEL: 1 CORINTHIANS 15:1-7

Now, brothers and sisters, I want to remind you of the gospel I preached to you, which you received and on which you have taken your stand. By this gospel you are saved, if you hold firmly to the word I preached to you. Otherwise, you have believed in vain. For what I received I passed on to you as of first importance: that Christ died for our sins according to the Scriptures, that he was buried, that he was raised on the third day according to the Scriptures, and that he appeared to Cephas, and then to the Twelve. After that, he appeared to more than five hundred of the brothers and sisters at the same time, most of whom are still living, though some have fallen asleep. Then he appeared to James, then to all the apostles.

JESUS IS THE WAY: JOHN 14:6

Jesus answered, "I am the way and the truth and the life. No one comes to the Father except through me."

ALL HAVE SINNED: ROMANS 3:23

For all have sinned and fall short of the glory of God.

SIN LEADS TO DEATH: ROMANS 6:23

For the wages of sin is death, but the gift of God is eternal life in Christ Jesus our Lord.

REPENT: ACTS 2:38

Peter replied, "Repent and be baptized, every one of you, in the name of Jesus Christ for the forgiveness of your sins. And you will receive the gift of the Holy Spirit."

BELIEVE: ROMANS 10:9

If you declare with your mouth, "Jesus is Lord," and believe in your heart that God raised him from the dead, you will be saved.

CONFESS: 1 JOHN 1:9

If we confess our sins, he is faithful and just and will forgive us our sins and purify us from all unrighteousness.

NEW LIFE: 2 CORINTHIANS 5:17

Therefore, if anyone is in Christ, the new creation has come: The old has gone, the new is here!

BAPTISM: ROMANS 6:1-7

What shall we say, then? Shall we go on sinning so that grace may increase? By no means! We are those who have died to sin; how can we live in it any longer? Or don't you know that all of us who were baptized into Christ Jesus were baptized into his death? We were therefore buried with him through baptism into death in order that, just as Christ was raised from the dead through the glory of the Father, we too may live a new life. For if we have been united with him in a death like his, we will certainly also be united with him in a resurrection like his. For we know that our old self was crucified with him so that the body ruled by sin might be done away with, that we should no longer be slaves to sin—because anyone who has died has been set free from sin.

Willie Robertson is best known for starring in and executive producing A&E's *Duck Dynasty*. He is a New York Times best-selling author of several books including *Gospeler*. He is the founder of Buck Commander and CEO of Duck Commander. Willie expanded his family's small business from a living room operation to a company for all things outdoors and has sold millions of duck calls and merchandise worldwide.

He appeared as the "Mallard" on *The Masked Singer* and in many other TV shows, movies, and platforms as himself. Willie also hosted a talk show and podcast. Willie has continued to be an avid outdoorsman and has founded a Sportsman Camp for young people at Camp Ch-Yo-Ca in Calhoun, LA.

While the Robertsons' story is an excellent example of entrepreneurship and dedication, it is at its core built on faith and family. Willie continues to teach the Gospel to tens of thousands of people worldwide. Willie and Korie live near their children and grandchildren in West Monroe, Louisiana, where he enjoys cooking the family meals.